Tasks Galore

Let's Play

Structured Steps to Social Engagement and Symbolic Play

Laurie Eckenrode, Pat Fennell, Kathy Hearsey, and Beth Reynold

Tasks Galore Let's Play

Fourth Book in a Series

Acknowledgments

During the three years it has taken to complete *Tasks Galore Let's Play*, we have been fortunate to share our time with many wonderful families and their beautiful children. Hearing the children's laughter and seeing their smiles have made all of us appreciate the power of play. We recognize and applaud the fact that play is indeed a wonderful avenue to learning. We thank each child and parent who enriched our lives.

In all of our books, Michelle Jordy's creative touch has helped us depict tasks much better. She eagerly accepted every graphic challenge we posed with astounding results. Her help is invaluable and we are thrilled she continues to be part of our team.

Teachers, Amanda Benson, Rebecca Crouch, Dorothy Evans, Mona Fulghum, Missy Hendrick, Jennifer Matzuga, and Susan Page welcomed us into their classrooms. We are grateful for the enthusiasm and experience each of them so graciously imparted to us. We admire the compassion and capabilities they demonstrate daily when working with their students.

Knowledge we gained initially from our colleagues at TEACCH is augmented by their ongoing willingness to problem solve with us on ways to enhance our teaching strategies. We are grateful for this dialogue that enlightens us.

We are privileged to have such a talented team of professionals who provide ongoing expertise and encouragement. We thank John Barton for his editorial guidance, Tim and Terry Davis of Landmark Printing for their graphic and design ideas, Doug Fennell for his photographic knowledge, Carolyn Perry-Jones for her structured teaching know-how, and Deborah Leisey for her artistry. We are appreciative of their talents, collaboration, and inspiration as we complete our latest book *Tasks Galore Let's Play*.

About the Authors

The authors utilized their abundant and varied knowledge, gained from working with students of different ages, diagnoses, and ability levels, to create *Tasks Galore Let's Play.* Their professional experiences with TEACCH (Treatment and Education of Autistic and related Communication handicapped Children), an evidence-based service, training, and research program at the University of North Carolina, has enabled them to be well-versed in structured teaching methodology.

Laurie Eckenrode, is a veteran teacher who served in the TEACCH demonstration classroom for elementary-aged students. She also served as a classroom trainer. Laurie is currently serving preschool-aged children with special needs in inclusive settings.

Pat Fennell was, formerly a teacher and program director in a developmental center for students with significant learning challenges. For twenty-one years, she worked with TEACCH, where she was a psycho-educational therapist, consultant, and classroom trainer.

Kathy Hearsey, also formerly a teacher in a TEACCH demonstration classroom for adolescents, works for TEACCH as a psycho-educational therapist, presenter and classroom trainer. She also served as the director of supported employment for TEACCH.

Beth Reynolds, is currently serving as the lead teacher for the TEACCH demonstration classroom for preschoolers and as a presenter and classroom trainer. Beth has also served as a community program instructor and activities director for the North Carolina Autism Society's summer camp program.

Laurie, Pat, Kathy, and Beth have provided training across the United States, as well as abroad. They have won many awards for their achievements in the field of special education.

Table Of Contents

INTRODUCTION

New studies link the growth of symbolic play in children with autism spectrum disorders (ASD) with positive changes in their social, language, and imitation skills. As educators, we sometimes bypass direct teaching of play skills as we conscientiously work on improving abilities that our young students eventually will need for academic learning and independent living. It is often easier for children with autism spectrum disorders to learn school skills, such as matching, counting, and reading, than it is for them to play naturally. In *Let's Play*, we want to change this focus and take advantage of the correlation between pretend play and cognitive development. Although we still work on cognitive, social, communicative, and imitative skills that will be needed in the future, play becomes the vehicle for that learning.

The communicative and social challenges that children with ASD confront have huge impacts on their aptitude for playing with others. These challenges hinder their early back-and-forth engagement with caregivers and complex role playing with peers. Children with ASD have a need for sameness, evident in their preferring to use toys in rigid and set patterns, and may have over interest or aversion to various sensory stimuli. These traits limit their toy interest and experimentation. By planning ahead, organizing steps sequentially, and thinking imaginatively, most children are able to integrate ideas easily into play scenarios - complete with props and different characters. The thinking skills necessary for such elaborate play, however, are the very ones that are problematic in children with ASD. Although play is hard work, we want our students to experience the joys of playing, while maintaining that it can have a significant effect on their future development.

The goal of the activities in *Let's Play* is not to teach play. Play is created and spontaneously initiated by the child; it cannot be taught. Yet, because quality play enhances overall learning, and, because children with ASD encounter learning differences that make the natural development of play skills extremely difficult, it is important to teach our students the tools or mechanisms that underlie play.

The authors of **_Let's Play_** present strategies for accomplishing such instruction. Our strategies begin with observing our students closely to assess their interests, current levels of play, and any rigid patterns. We then determine which new play skills the students are ready to learn and how to incorporate their interests, while encouraging flexibility. When directly teaching new skills, we help students establish productive routines. We also supplement our verbal prompts and gestures with visual ones and directly teach the students to notice and respond to these cues independently. The visual cues eventually can be used as reminders in natural settings with peers when we are not facilitating the play. We continually monitor our students' play development by pinpointing ongoing areas of need and sharing delight in their playtime successes. The chapters in **_Let's Play_**,

- People Can Be Fun,
- It's a Toy,
- Managing Play Times,
- Making Choices and Ending Them,
- It's Pretend,
- It's a Playmate, and
- Remembering the Structure in Popular Toys and Games

illustrate with text and pictures the practical application of these strategies.

CHAPTER 1
PEOPLE CAN BE FUN

Parents eagerly await their infants' first smiles and directed eye gazes; they delight in hearing their babies' laughter after tickle and peek-a-boo games. Infants and toddlers discover their first playmates because parents are the source of so much fun. Children who struggle with social and communication challenges, however, may find objects more fascinating than people because things have unchanging details and predictable actions. For these children, people may be too variable and confusing to be fun. Our work in helping children with developmental differences play more successfully, thus, begins with giving them reasons to attend to us, ensuring our actions are fun, and sharing their enjoyment enthusiastically.

To teach children what fun it can be to play with others and to encourage their person engagement and joint attention, consider
- joining children in actions they initiate and find fun,
- creating anticipation routines,
- making ourselves essential in fun games,
- incorporating sounds,
- exaggerating reactions, and
- adding surprises to familiar routines.

JOINING CHILDREN IN ACTIONS THEY INITIATE AND FIND FUN

These teachers find great value in observing what their students view as fun. They frequently follow a student's lead because they recognize that joining children at their skill and interest levels may eventually lead to joint social engagement.

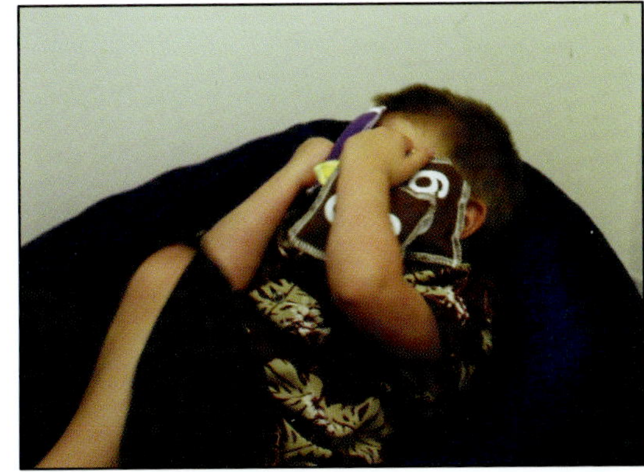

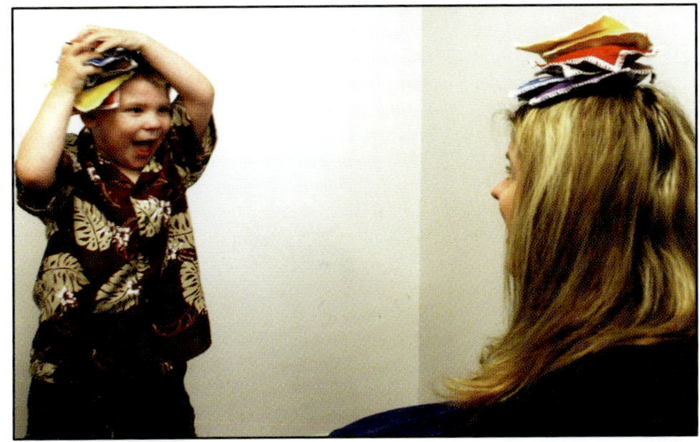

To encourage this student to pay attention to others, his teacher copied his activities. When he was enjoying putting pop beads on his fingers, his teacher joined him and did the same activity. The child's attention moved from his fingers to those of the teacher as he learned to share an experience with someone else.

Another teacher wanted her student to use alphabet bean bags to work on academic goals, but he had no interest. When she allowed him to play with the bean bags as he wished, the teacher saw his enjoyment in stacking them on his head. She copied his idea to the student's delight. She recognized that social engagement was also an important goal for this student. The teacher abandoned the academic goal temporarily to join in with an activity her student deemed fun and shared his enjoyment. In doing so, she drew attention to herself and helped her student have fun with someone, not just with things.

Sometimes a child has a favorite action that he frequently incorporates into his play. This teacher noted how much her student enjoyed crashing materials. She figured out a way to incorporate this self-initiated action into an activity of shared enjoyment. Her student followed along as she read the nursery rhyme about Humpty Dumpty. At the end of the rhyme, they both fell down, just as Humpty had a great fall. While joining him in his favorite action, the teacher taught her student both about nursery rhymes and shared enjoyment. Together they had fun.

This teacher realizes that some of her students paid attention better to joining in when she structured play with specific toys at a table. In this less distracting setting, she provides the same toys for both her and her student. First, she gives her student an orange tube and imitates his actions with her matching yellow tube. Next, she places two pairs of sunglasses on the table and waits and watches to discover what her student will do with them. Once he uses them, she copies whatever he does and waits for him to notice, so they can have fun together.

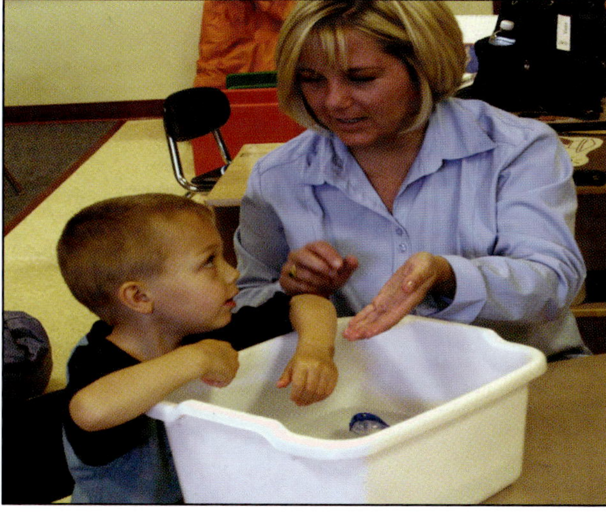

This mother finds ways to join in when her son plays in water. She gives him wind up toys that require her help. Using an upturned palm gesture, she encourages him to seek her assistance. She heightens her child's enjoyment by adding ideas, such as a flying whale that stirs up ripples and sounds when splashing into the water. The child keeps his mother as part of the fun by requesting help and for the whale to fly and splash again. While the child is so engaged, the parent or teacher is thinking about what next step to add to advance person-engagement skills.

CREATING ANTICIPATION ROUTINES

An aspect of early fun in social games is the element of surprise, which appeals to children's natural sense of wonder. Sometimes, children with learning difficulties do not know to focus their attention on the caregiver as they await and anticipate some fun surprise to occur. Using anticipation routines draws attention to us. Anticipation helps children become engaged, first, with us and, then, with the pleasurable activity that follows. We become fun because we are part of the first/next sequence.

A routine that includes saying the same words, having the same excited affect, and making the same gestures increases the child's attention to us. First, while smiling broadly and excitedly saying the word, "tickle," this teacher creeps her fingers toward the student. The child waits and watches her teacher because she has experienced this routine many times and anticipates the tickle and hug that will follow. Over time, the teacher gradually pauses after saying the word and slowly creeps her fingers towards the child so the child's focus to both the game and the teacher lengthens and her anticipation intensifies. Adding pauses and changing the speed lead to greater surprise because the child is not sure when she will be tickled. The teacher matches the child's enthusiasm, so they both express enjoyment of tickling and being tickled.

Holding up a toy and saying words excitedly and quickly, such as "Ready, go!" draw this student's attention from the toy to his teacher. With repeated practice, he learns that the rhythmic words provide the precursor for the result he is eager to see, a car rolling down a chute. Over time, the teacher's actions in the anticipation routine become as pleasurable as the toy action. We give the child another experience to learn what fun we can be.

First, finding Mommy and, then, getting hugs and tickles is another surprise game that children love. Children with ASD, however, will enjoy the game most if words said, affect shown, and surprise resulting are repeated often. Once we notice what reactions (e.g., tickles, hugs, tosses in the air, etc.) the child finds enticing, we can make these part of anticipation routines. Knowing his Mommy will say, "Boo," smile animatedly, and tickle him enables this student to focus better on his search to find her.

MAKING OURSELVES ESSENTIAL IN FUN GAMES

We create enjoyable play activities that cannot happen without us. By becoming necessary, children associate us with the fun.

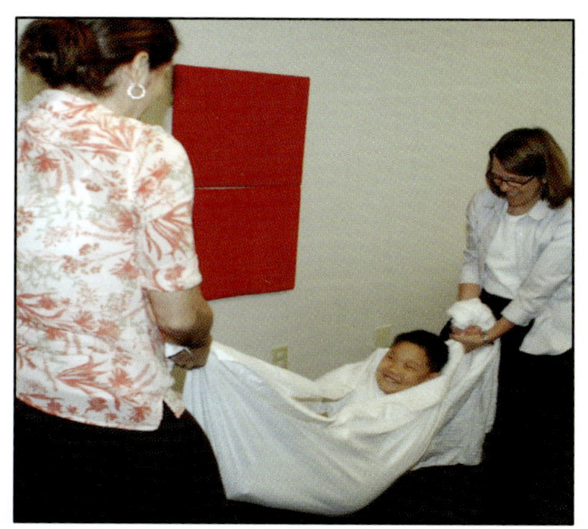

One student loves vestibular movement, but swinging in a blanket is not possible without his two teachers. He gives a representational object, a knotted white napkin, to a teacher to request a swing; then he engages further by exchanging eye gazes and smiles with her.

Another student loves rocking in the wooden boat. His teacher activates the motion while situated in front of the child. Her student notices her happiness and expresses his enjoyment through looks and smiles.

Discovering her daughter loves piggy-back rides, this mother becomes essential for the fun to happen. Such movement games are a great way to engage jointly with our students. Asking parents how they have fun with the children at home gives us ideas for engaging the students at school. Helping students see how people can be fun lays important groundwork for back-and-forth interactions.

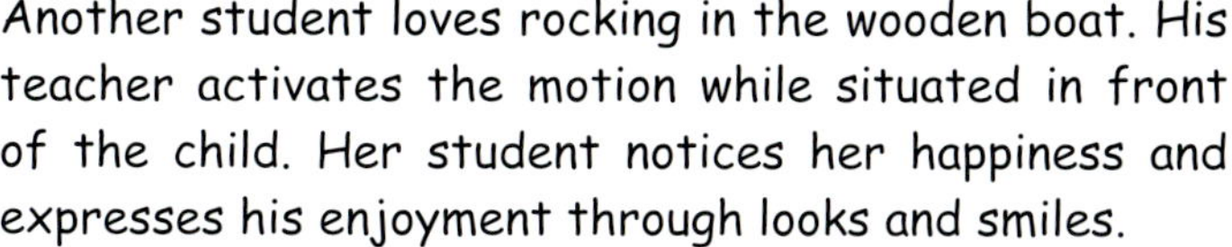

What could be more fun to most small children than a high-flying airplane game! Established routines, such as wearing pink socks when it is time to fly, help children shift attention from fascinating objects to fun people. Seeing the pink socks helps them know when to ask for airplane rides. When his teacher is not wearing the pink socks, the student knows then is not the time to have a ride. Because the movement game requires an adult, this student learns to associate a fun time with a fun person. He and his teacher become playmates.

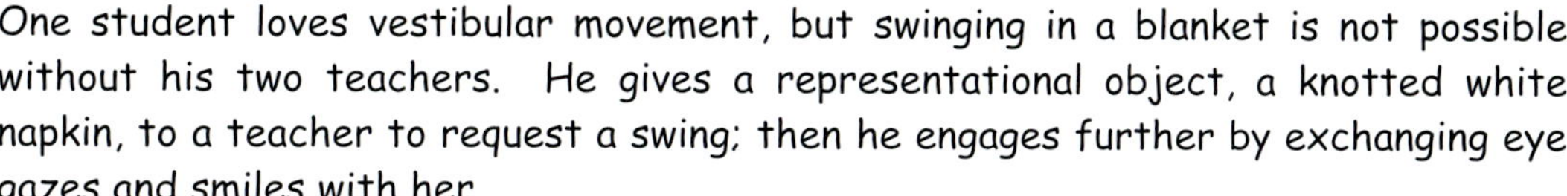

INCORPORATING SOUNDS

Sounds capture our attention and make us laugh. These teachers try out different sounds with their students. Because students find the teachers' sound interesting, they make eye contact, copy the sounds, and engage with their teachers.

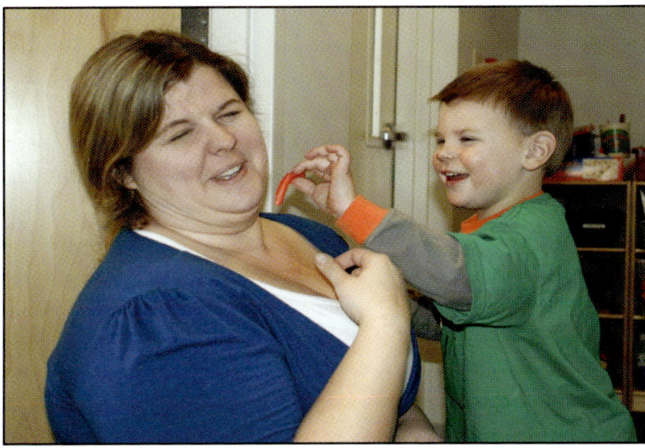

Sounds associated with eating and drinking are understandable as well as fun. This teacher and her student make exaggerated "Ahhhh" sounds after the toy drinks.

Another student loves his teacher's yucky sound when he suggests she eat a worm.

Here, the teacher makes galloping sounds as her student puts the horse into a barn in hopes that he will notice the sound, enjoy it, and connect his teacher with the fun sound.

This teacher uses a big metal pot with lids inside to create fun sounds when bean bags drop on top of them. Dropping bean bags from their heads, instead of just tossing the toys into the pot, is even funnier, and the student shares his experience through eye contact, smiles, and gestures.

EXAGGERATING REACTIONS

Sometimes, we exaggerate our reactions as we attempt to draw students' attention from objects. Our amplified reactions increase the likelihood that the children will notice us. Responding to children's actions with our enthusiastic and excited reactions often helps them more readily express and share their own enthusiasm. Although exaggerating our affect intrigues most students, we do watch cautiously for students who may withdraw from such displays. As with all strategies, we adjust our actions and reactions to fit the needs of the individual child.

One teacher exaggerates her surprised expression when the spider appears to frighten Miss Muffet away. Because she gets so excited, her student's focus shifts from the spider toy to her.

A teacher smiles happily on seeing her student emerge from a tunnel. Her student realizes that it is fun to be with others when they express their enjoyment so clearly.

After a student accidentally spills rice while making a noise-making shaker, his teacher laughs heartedly. This laughter engages her student, so that he makes eye contact and laughs too.

ADDING SURPRISES TO FAMILIAR ROUTINES

Adding changes to known routines is a great strategy for introducing surprises. The best part about being surprised is to verify that others notice, so you can share the feeling. This is another wonderful way to have fun with others.

Some children find great delight in playing peek-a-boo by pulling a blanket off the other person's face. This student did not expect to see a big, blue nose when she uncovered her teacher's face. The surprise extended the length of time she attended and engaged with her teacher.

To complete a puzzle, this student must roll a dump truck to his teacher and wait for her to fill it with a puzzle piece before rolling it back to him. In this back-and-forth game, he learns about turn taking. On the day she puts in a piece that does not fit his puzzle, however, he learns about joint attention. His expression reflects his surprise as he waits for his teacher to acknowledge the misstep. Recognizing the silliness in such surprises helps our students develop their senses of humor.

 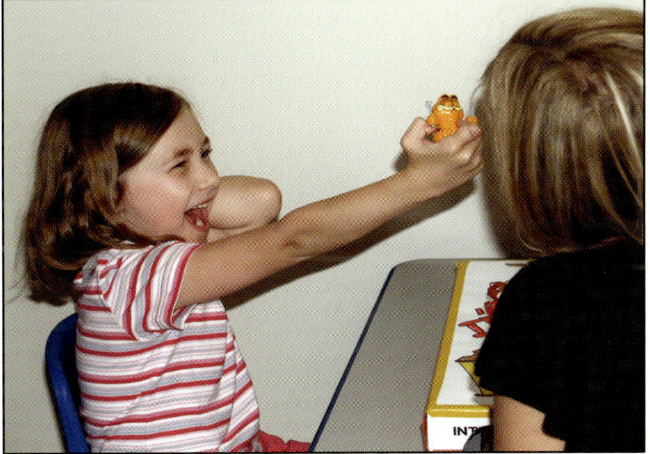

Children often want to share the surprise when something unpredictable happens. Here the student is retelling the story of The Three Bears. Hidden under Papa Bear's bed in the cutout box lid is not a bear or Goldilocks but the cartoon character Garfield™. Because the student is shocked to find something unexpected, she laughs and shares her surprise. Changing the familiar leads to person-engagement and gives the child another lesson in how much fun she can have with people.

CHAPTER 2
IT'S A TOY

There are so many wonderful toys. Children with developmental challenges may glance at a toy, even touch it, yet, not play with it. They may not yet have developed readiness in their visual-motor or cognitive skills to know how to understand a toy beyond its sensory properties; they may not find it interesting; they may not know how to organize its pieces; or they may be unable to sustain their attention through a sequence of steps. Additionally, children with ASD may over focus on one toy, object, or activity and attend to it exclusively and resist trying out new play materials. They may over focus on one detail of a toy and not experiment with what happens when toys are used in different ways. All these reasons limit the richness and variety of the children's toy play. Many of our students, therefore, are unable to utilize the potential of toys to teach them important cognitive lessons that underlie more advanced learning. It is important that we develop strategies to teach students both how to use toys appropriately and how to attend to something new and different.

To help children experience what toys have to offer, consider
- creating toy appeal
  - include students' interests and strengths,
  - personalize toys,
  - use familiar routines, and
  - use words or scripts,
- organizing toys so they are ready to play
  - stabilize into one container,
  - segment pieces,
  - use containers to organize parts, and
  - highlight an important feature,
- visually clarifying how to use toys
  - do what and how, and
  - how long/concept of finished,
- providing visual instructions for toy setup, and
- creating opportunities for "what if" exploration.

CREATING TOY APPEAL

We want our students to see novel toys and be enticed to notice and play with them. We attempt to make a toy appealing to the children by incorporating strengths and interests and making toys personal. We also look for familiar routines that can become part of toy designs.

INCLUDE STUDENTS' INTERESTS AND STRENGTHS

Students' interests may include favorite characters, sensory experiences, or even movement. Sometimes, their interests are also their areas of strength. Many children find numbers and letters quite appealing. Not only does accommodating the children's strengths and interests capture their attention but also enables them to feel more confident when learning new play skills or playing with unfamiliar materials.

This student loves tactile play. His interest is evident in his overfocus on these types of materials to the exclusion of others. Instead of disregarding this interest when we try to teach the student to attend to something different, however, we utilize the interest. He finds colorful noisemakers when enjoying a tactile experience. He pauses to attend to these and begins to add visual and auditory exploration to his repertoire of skills.

In contrast, we design toy play for another student who has a strong interest in puzzles but does not like tactile play. Because she is motivated to finish the puzzle, she is willing to reach into the bin of dried beans to find the pieces.

A student's willingness to pay attention to a Play-doh task occurs when we design a task using his favorite characters. Here, he cuts a cat out of blue Play-doh, a tree out of green, and a butterfly out of yellow to follow written directions on the picture. Incorporating his beloved characters on the picture heightens his engagement with the toy.

It is appealing and meaningful for children to build with Duplos™ when doing so creates their favorite characters.

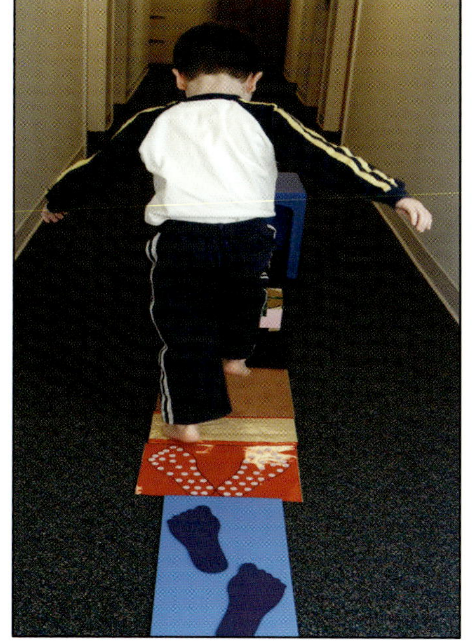

Some students may shy away from noise-making activities. We increase the appeal of a xylophone when we design the musical activity so the student uses thin wooden sticks instead of a mallet, creating a softer sound. Too, we attach pictures of the student's favorite characters as an additional way to draw his attention, interest, and acceptance. He chooses a cartoon stick, plays a note, and then places it in the character's space ship.

Interest in animals provides a good reason for another student to color. Incorporating this attraction makes using markers much more pleasing.

Sometimes, we use the interests of our students at the end of a sequence. For example, here, we set up a play activity for students to walk on a textured path with their bare feet. Because this will be a new experience for many of our students, we add a toy of high interest at the end. This student finds a favorite ball after he walks the textured path. Each step along the path has a different texture ranging from sand paper to Velcro dots to sticky paper. The excitement of getting his favorite toy decreases his apprehension about his feet touching unusual textures.

Many of our students recognize letters and numbers and delight in these academic strengths and interests. We frequently think about how we can use their number and letter interests and skills in our toy designs. For example, numbers might indicate either a sequence or a quantity.

One student willingly tries to catch a fish with a net because we number each fish and have a colored, numbered template to show where to place the fish.

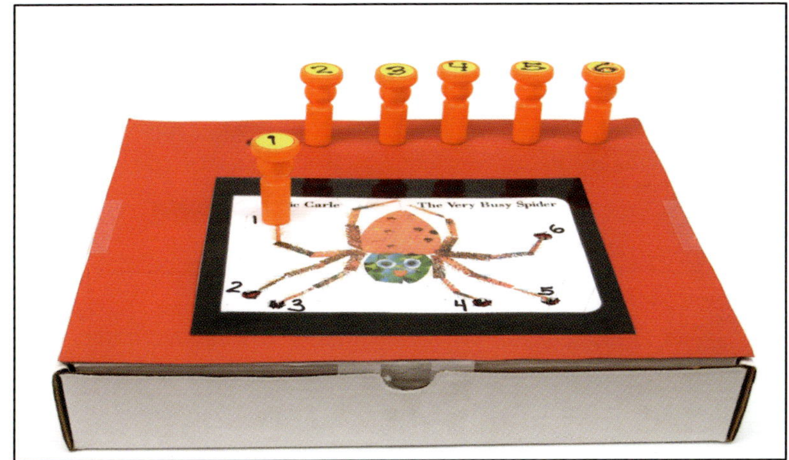

A teacher-made pegboard combines the interest of counting with a familiar story book.

Creating musical sounds using rhythm sticks to tap out syllables in a written word combines a play activity with an interest in reading. The students say the word and hit their sticks for each syllable as their teacher points to it.

Some students find making music more enjoyable when combined with their number interests. They beat their teacher-made bongos the number of times indicated.

PERSONALIZE TOYS

Children enjoy toys that are about them, their possessions, or people who are important in their lives. Toys or activities that include these personal aspects draw their attention because they see pictures or hear words that are familiar. This familiarity increases the toy's appeal.

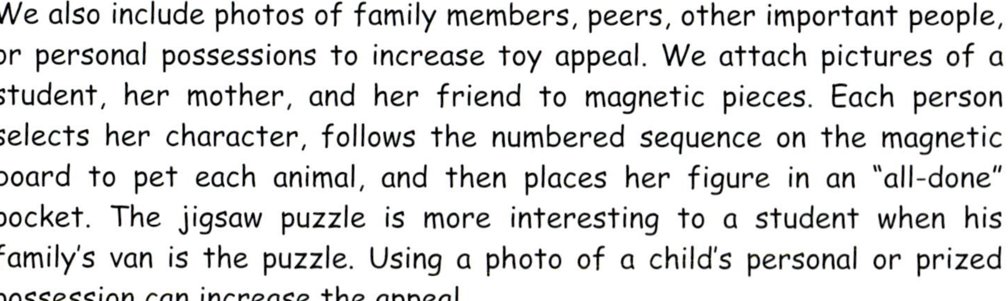

One technique is to add the student's photo to a toy. one child pushes rattling balls through a tall tube. Seeing his picture on these balls and hearing his teacher's excited expressions about watching Johnny fall down the tube draw his attention more readily. In a book with lift-up flaps, we superimpose another child's pictures over those in the book. She finds her photos while hearing a story about her being in the tub, behind the door, and fast asleep. Seeing themselves in a picture book creates appeal for many students.

We also include photos of family members, peers, other important people, or personal possessions to increase toy appeal. We attach pictures of a student, her mother, and her friend to magnetic pieces. Each person selects her character, follows the numbered sequence on the magnetic board to pet each animal, and then places her figure in an "all-done" pocket. The jigsaw puzzle is more interesting to a student when his family's van is the puzzle. Using a photo of a child's personal or prized possession can increase the appeal.

For our students, personalizing a toy with their own everyday experiences makes abstractions seem real and creates the desire to engage. Pretending to drive a bus to school becomes more understandable and appealing when toy figures are picked up from houses labeled with classmates' photos.

Photos in an album help another student recall a real-life adventure. This picture shows his riding an amusement park airplane; we provide representative toys, so he can act out his personal experience.

We think about familiar routines that children use frequently and how we can incorporate some of these into our toy designs. Routines can add predictability. Knowing what to expect and feeling competent to tackle an activity always increases appeal.

  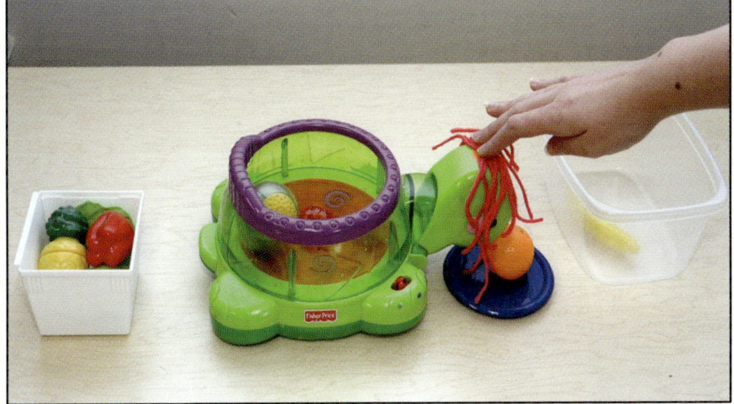

Putting something inside something else is a meaningful routine for our students. One student found toys meaningless and somewhat aversive; however, this same student successfully put items into containers during work sessions. Once she learned the put-in routine with the puff balls, her teacher gradually altered the container with a circus theme and, next, changed the puff balls to circus animals. Making these step-by-step changes to a familiar routine enabled the student to try toy materials and eventually enjoy playing with circus-themed toys.

We designed an activity with this toy turtle that includes a familiar eating routine. The student initially attends to this cause-and-effect toy to feed the turtle. How to activate the toy becomes more obvious when we add colorful yarn to the head. The student pushes the turtle's head down to eat food on the plate and says, "Yum, yum." By carrying out what is familiar, he learns something new: that the balls on the turtle's back spin

Putting materials into containers is a familiar routine for this student. While lying on a big ball, he puts colorful plastic eggs into a container. Combining the put-in routine, a skill about which he feels confident, with the big ball and an unusual position eases him into this different experience.

USE WORDS OR SCRIPTS

When we first teach children how to use a toy, we include language cues and encourage those children who are ready to include these words in their play. We find lhat rhythmic language can help organize children's interest and attention to toys and create greater appeal.

This girl practices fine motor maneuvers necessary to activate a busy box toy while also learning the words associated with her actions.

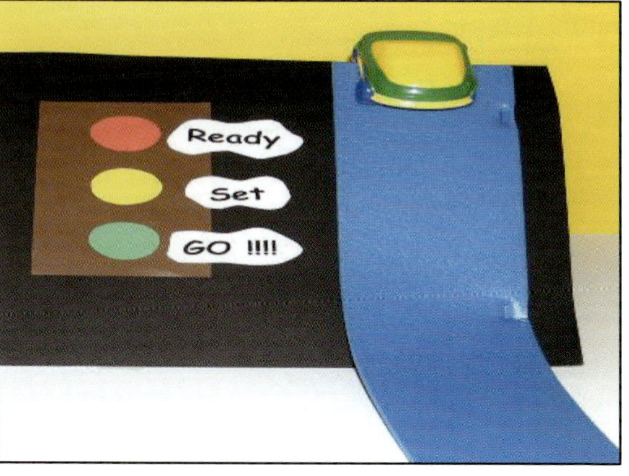

Learning to associate "Ready, Set, Go!" with this teacher-made car track makes it clearer when to begin and, thus, the play more enticing.

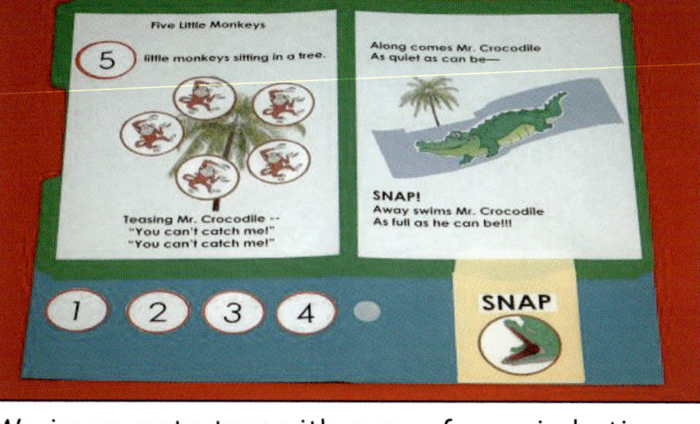

Adding the "Oops, I missed" box to this catapulting game gives students a clear place for pieces to go when they do not land in the frog's mouth. Additionally, the "Oops, I missed" phrase provides a mantra or definite verbal response to a potentially frustrating situation. Savvy teachers will model how getting to use the "Oops, I missed" box and saying the words can be as much fun as getting a piece in the mouth. No longer do the students think they make a mistake when they miss.

We incorporate toys with many of our circle time routines. One teacher depicts the rhyme, "Five Little Monkeys," with pictures, numbers, and words. In addition to repeating the rhyme, each student takes a turn becoming "Mr. Alligator" and pulling a stuffed monkey from the tree. Because the rhyme is familiar, using puppets becomes more appealing.

Knocking items over to see them fall down can be exciting for some children. By using language to organize their attention, they are able to independently set up toys to be pushed down. Children align the shapes by matching colors. Language prompts help them to know what to say when all go falling down. These same visual prompts that remind students what to say generalizes to other play activities, such as knocking down building blocks.

When playing with the farm, students choose a card that tells them to which animal to say good night. A repetitive verbal script supported by visual cues enhances the students' desire to play with the toy because now they know what to do and saying, "Night, night, pig; night, night, chicken," etc., and then putting the animal to bed in the barn keeps them engaged.

ORGANIZING TOYS SO THEY ARE READY TO PLAY

When the children are learning about toys, it is essential that they judge them to be interesting and understandable on first glance. If they must think about how to gather all the toy pieces and organize them, they are unlikely to engage quickly. We attempt to organize toys so that our students view them as ready to play and not walk away without first giving them a try. Techniques we use when presenting toys so they appear ready to play include stabilizing pieces, using containers to organize pieces, separating pieces, and highlighting a detail or any visual instructions. We decide what organization children might need by watching them interact with various play materials.

STABILIZE INTO ONE CONTAINER: It is frustrating when we try to play and the pieces topple over, fall off, or roll away.

This student can play with water independently because her teacher stabilized a bin of water onto this large lid.

This ring stack comes ready to play in its bin with the post glued down and the rings inside a partial container. The student does not have to locate or keep up with the pieces to play with the ring stack.

SEGMENT PIECES: Some children may flip, stack, sort, or line up multiple pieces without understanding the purpose of a toy. If we separate pieces, it often becomes much easier for students to see what to do and for how long. They can then quickly engage without being distracted by the parts.

For this dinosaur puzzle, cardboard pieces stand up in slits cut into a box, so little hands can easily pick them up.

The other activity separates the toy cars in an array rather than placing them all in a container from which the student might be apt to grab several cars at one time. Students pick up one car, place it at the top of the ramp, and watch as it rolls into the opening after they let the car go. All the action is contained on top of a shoe box and ready to play.

USE CONTAINERS TO ORGANIZE PARTS: Organizing pieces into containers helps students know where to focus their attention to find the relevant pieces.

In this task, we use a plastic tray to contain all the parts of the activity. Students pick one of the balls that we separate into muffin tin sections. They spin the balls in the black bowl and place it in the tall tube when finished. Tin, bowl, and tube are affixed to the tray to prevent spills.

Seeing a self-contained toy, such as this large container with two cars, encourages students to start playing. They do not have to think about where to play with their cars, and the cars are easy to retrieve when they stop and need to be restarted.

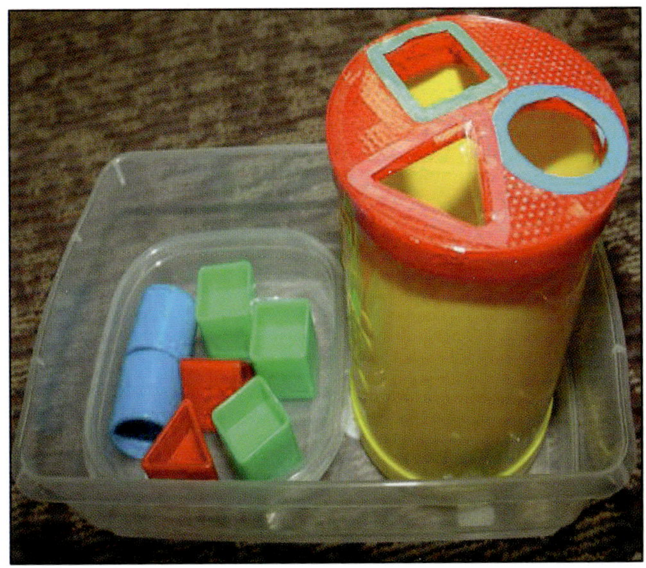

It is more meaningful to many of our students to play with a toy if they do not first have to take it apart. Taking apart and then putting it back together often makes no sense to them. Shapes are ready to go into the shape box. The student does not have to organize any of the pieces.

Clothes are ready to put on the doll; this toy is ready to play.

HIGHLIGHT AN IMPORTANT FEATURE: For many students, simply highlighting a feature of a toy draws their attention to an important aspect.

Putting a large colored disk on the push-down button of a top helps the student know where to place his hand to activate the toy.

A large plastic oval on the string of a pull toy shows this girl where to place her hands or fingers. Highlighting cues make some toys ready to play.

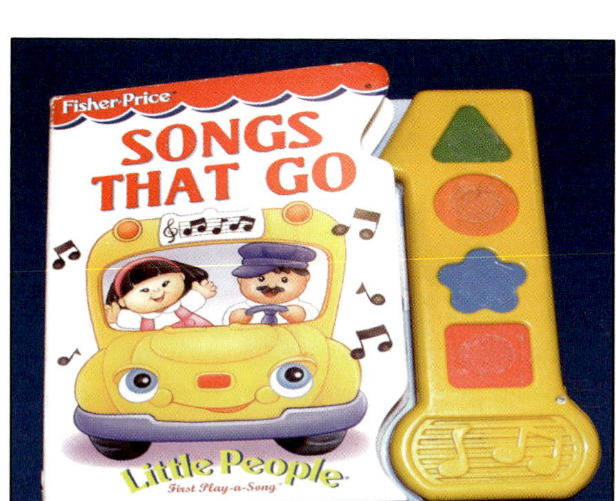

Sound books have multiple buttons that make noise, but it is often difficult for the child to know which button corresponds to which page. Covering the extra buttons and placing a matching picture over the corresponding button on the panel of a sound book helps the child make the connection between the sounds and the action pictures.

Placing the visual instruction on top of the play materials highlights the importance of this information so the student can quickly become involved in block play.

VISUALLY CLARIFYING HOW TO USE TOYS

Now that we have made toys appealing so they capture our students' attention and have organized pieces so toys appear ready to play, we next must help students understand how to use them appropriately or in a meaningful way. Because most of our students have good visual skills, we often use visual strategies to answer the questions of what/how to play, and how long to play. If we provide comprehensible answers to these questions, our students find it meaningful to use the toy as it is designed to be used. We match the visual method to the students' understanding. We take the extra time to adapt toys in individualized ways because we want our students to have mastery over toys and to feel proud of their accomplishments. Clarifying visually what and how much to do encourages students to finish. Achieving the goal of completing play activities means students understand the important concept of finishing and apply its importance once they eventually confront school tasks and daily chores.

Note how confusing some store-bought toys must be for students with developmental problems because there are so many different activities within. This store-bought tool kit includes activities for: hammering, placing shapes into a shape sorter, and twisting/turning nuts on bolts. It would be unclear for many children with ASD to know where to begin, what to do, or when they would be finished. Sometimes, it is necessary to simplify a toy by highlighting the answer of what or how to play.

Adapted toys initially isolate skills to clarify and simplify visually what to do and for how long.   In one activity, the child hammers each peg until it falls into the box. In a separate activity, the child unscrews each wooden bolt and places it into the cutout. As the child learns to play using the separate skills, next, toys might incorporate multiple skills. In the third teacher-made toy, the student uses the attached tools to hammer the pegs into the Styrofoam, twist the nuts off of the bolts, and screw the bolts into the box. These toys are stabilized and set up, ready to play.

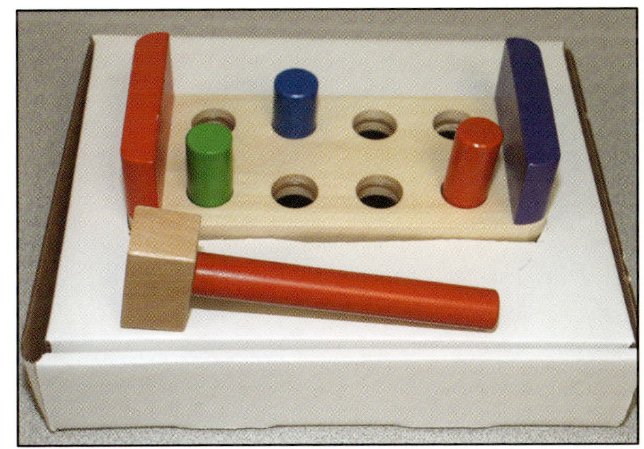
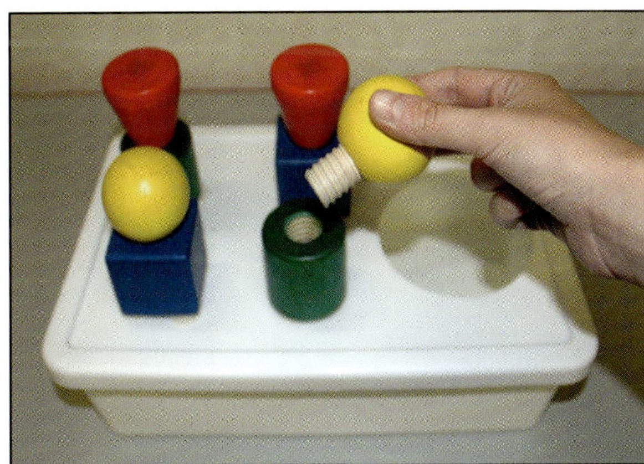
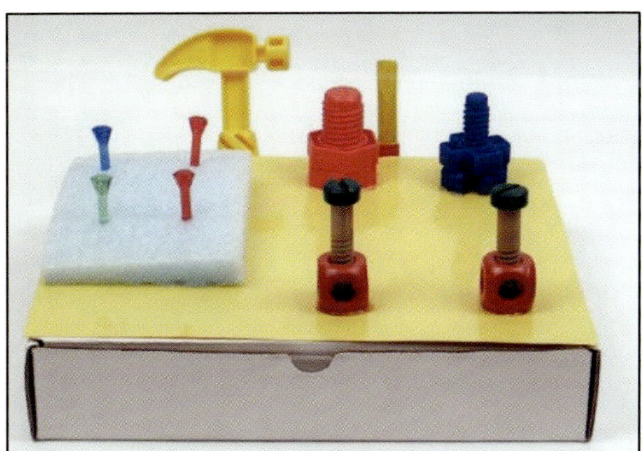

Sometimes the child questions, "What do I do with these materials?" Visual instructions provided with toys can give the answer. One child with ASD might simply be unfamiliar with the materials, and the visual instruction clarifies what to do. Others may already use the materials but in a rigid or inflexible manner and need visual supports to learn new play ideas with these toys. These visual instructions typically incorporate the individual's strengths in the areas of putting-in/on, matching, following a numbered sequence, or reading.

Some store-bought toys, such as puzzles, inherently provide the answer to the question, what to do. It is clear to many children to put the pieces into their places; the fit clarifies the accuracy of the placement.

For other toys, such as Mr. Potato Head™, however, there is nothing to clarify the accuracy of the placement. Placing a scanned photo of each piece onto Mr. Potato Head™ helps the student know where to put each piece through the match.

The visual instructions help the student play with a goal in mind. Changing the visual cue from one construction to the next encourages flexibility.

A student might not understand that these foam pieces can form a train without the visual directions that provide number and shape matches.

Another student might stack, line up, or sort blocks but without any end product. The scanned photos clarify for the student what to do with the Duplos™.

A student might play with a tiger on the mountain but with limited ideas. The flip book provides suggestions for the variety of ways to play with the tiger: slide, swim, climb, etc.

HOW LONG – CONCEPT OF FINISHED

Children often play with toys in a fluid manner, moving back and forth in the process without a clear expectation of finishing. But for many children with ASD, it is difficult to stay engaged without a view of the end in sight. Organizing toys so that they have a clear beginning and end is a strong engagement principle. At its simplest, children understand the concept of finished when everything is together. There are a variety of strategies for creating a concept of finished. For some toys, the materials are all in their places, such as the pieces in a puzzle or objects on the lotto board, but, for other toys, we have to create a "finished place."

The children know they are finished sliding the characters down the slide when all of the characters have disappeared into the cutout on the box. For many children, all gone or out of sight is the clearest concept of finished.

Another student playing bug lotto, understands that she is finished collecting the bugs out of the leaves when there is a matching plastic bug on each scanned photo.

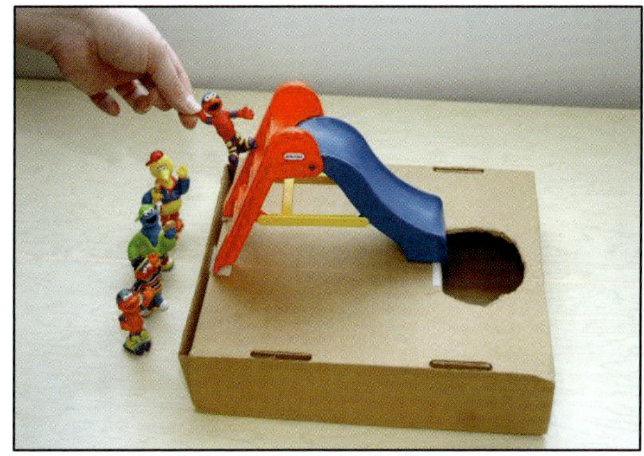

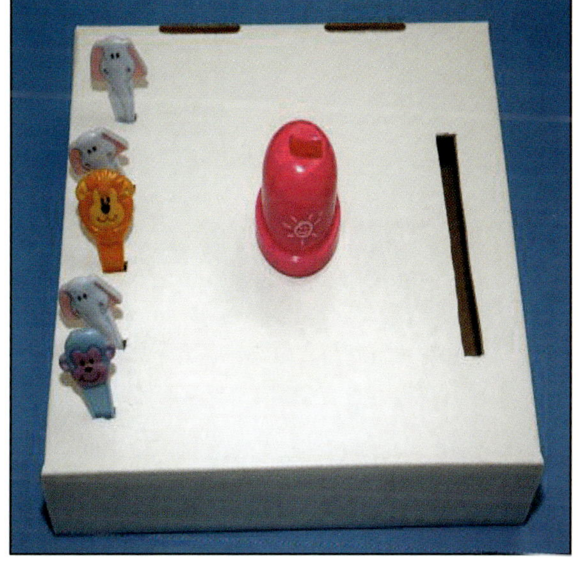

For many toys, there is no clear concept of finished, so it is necessary to create a visual system that helps the students know how long they will play with the toy. For bubbles, this young boy knows he blows bubbles with each wand. He is finished when he has blown bubbles with each wand, one at a time, and the wands are all placed into the "finished place" slot on the box.

PROVIDING VISUAL INSTRUCTIONS FOR TOY SETUP

When students are ready, we teach them how to set up their own toys. Just as we used visual cues to answer what to do with toys, we use visual cues to answer how to organize toys for play. Toys with multiple pieces often require setup as one plays or, in some instances, setup prior to beginning play. Providing the student with a strategy for setting up the pieces helps them engage with the toy more quickly and also increases their independence and sense of competence as they play. Teachers used various visual cues as instructions. Some of these cues correspond to the student's interest or strength in matching words and numbers.

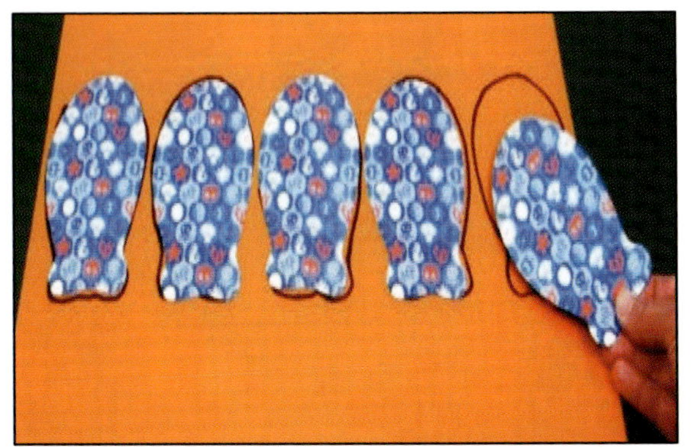

Students cannot turn the gears in this toy unless they place gears, so that they connect. Providing visual matches for gear placement enables students to set up this toy for successful play.

This teacher has drawn outlines of cards that aid students in dealing a hand of five for a game of Go Fish. The student can deal the cards using one-to-one correspondence.

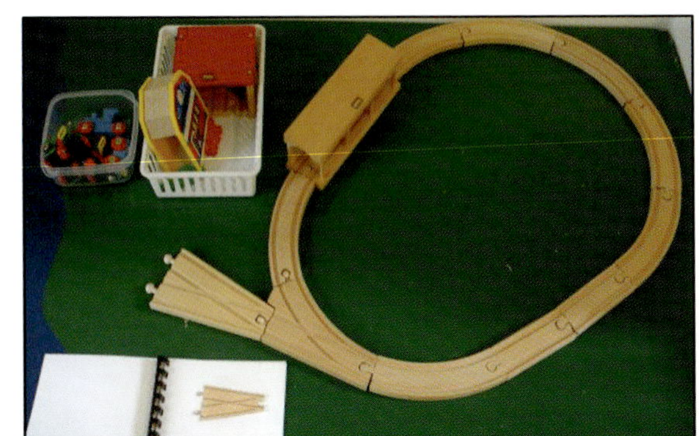

To set up furniture for doll house play, students match the furnishings to the words and pictures glued onto the floor in the corresponding "rooms."

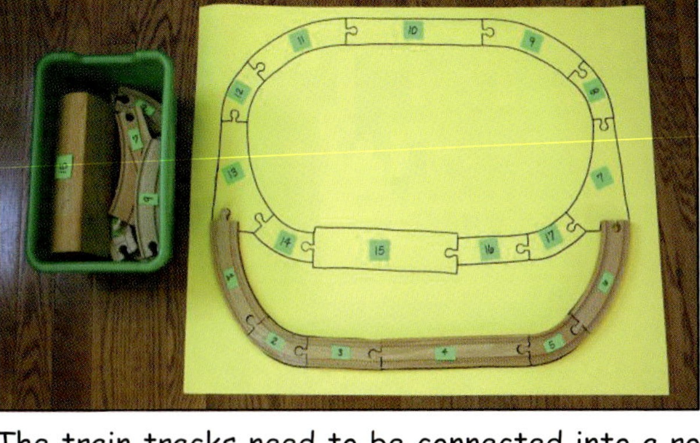

The train tracks need to be connected into a route before children can play with the train. We place number stickers on the track pieces for the students to match to the same numbers on the track drawn on the yellow board. For other students, we provide them with flip-book instructions for setting up their tracks. They find the piece depicted, link it with other pieces, and then turn the page to find what track piece comes next. As the child learns these strategies, they can choose among multiple track layout options.

Because they do not know how to arrange toys, students may never take this play farm from the shelf. Leaving the toy set up is not an option because it would take up too much space. If we provide them with meaningful visual cues for setup, such as this matching template, it will be clear to them how to organize the toy for farm play. For another farm, the setup might be to match the animals to their corresponding sounds.

Bowling is a game that requires ongoing setup for a student to stay engaged for an extended period of time. Students can play this bowling game independently because pictured visual instructions let them know where and how to set up the animal pins.

CREATING OPPORTUNITIES FOR "WHAT IF" EXPLORATION

Most children have what if ideas and experiment with these in their toy play. Because children with ASD have difficulty thinking in these original and flexible ways, we set up situations for them to realize how toys can be used in different ways and to test how properties of objects vary.

After students learn to use a hammer to knock the balls down the track and out the opening, we suggest there are other hammers that could work the same way. Here, the student experiments with each hammer and sees they all work.

Here, a student makes a necklace out of beads for her teddy bear. Before she saw playing with Teddy and stringing beads as separate activities, but now she experiments with combining ideas in new ways.

This student became familiar with putting numbered crayons into this pull toy at his work table. His teacher encourages him to use the pull dimension of the toy by placing crayons in a hallway. He explores ideas about what if I pull the toy to the crayon and learns how to be more efficient in loading his vehicle.

After learning to send cars down the track, this student's teacher has new ideas for him to try out. He finds that marbles roll down the track just as the cars did, and cars can roll down a slanted block just as they rolled down the track. Using toys in different ways is an important skill.

  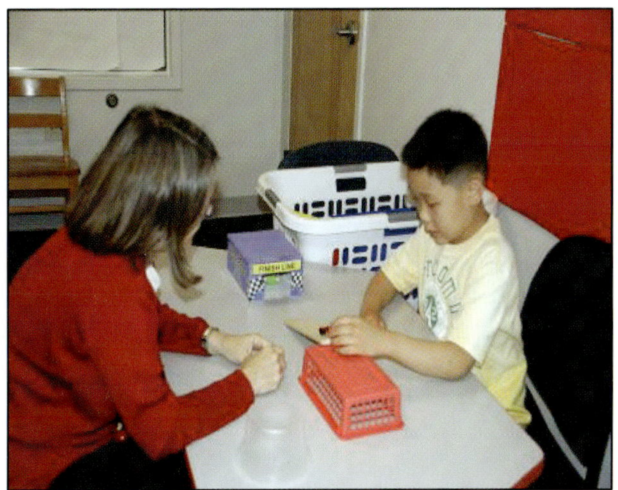

This boy learned how to stack blocks and now asks what else might stack. Here, he figures out that stacking works with fruits, too.

We set up this water table so our students can explore properties of objects. To help the students recognize the possibilities, we categorized the water toys by properties. The students can experiment with objects to determine whether they pour, squeeze, float, or swim.

CHAPTER 3
MANAGING PLAYTIMES

Once students know how to play with several different toys, it is time for them to learn how to manage play times. Typically children do not play with only a single toy during these times. Spontaneous play usually involves choosing a toy and then exploring a different one. Transitions between toys are effortless. Initiating play to focus on one activity in a meaningful way and, then, shifting that focus to another, however, can be a daunting task for students with developmental challenges. Further complicating play times for students with ASD is that they often are most comfortable playing repetitively with the same toy.

If our students are unresponsive to efforts to help them play more flexibly or cannot focus on any toy easily, we design play to-do lists for them, so they are able to maximize their playtimes for learning. These lists can guide the students, while playing independently, to use toys appropriately, expand their toy choices, and include symbolic ideas. The lists also stress sequencing and flexibility, skills needed when children play with peers. Lists, furthermore, help students understand that toys are discrete, and that play with them has beginning and ending points. Using a to-do list involves organizational strategies, such as selecting a toy, playing with it until finished, putting it away, and then selecting another. The lists indicate for beginning toy players what to play with, when they will be finished, and what happens next. With these things understood, students with social and communicative challenges participate more willingly. Our hope is that the students internalize these organizational strategies and, eventually, develop their own to-do lists when playing spontaneously, completing school lessons, and doing everyday chores.

We work with some students who do not need such lists because they play in an organized fashion with a variety of toys. Even these students, however, often benefit from visual information in their centers that helps them initiate play independently.

To help students utilize their playtimes for learning, consider
- teaching students how to use play sequences
  - teach the concept of first/next,
  - emphasize all done and putting away,
  - encourage students to use play sequences independently,
- assessing students' need for individual play spaces,
- enhancing learning through play lists in classroom centers,
- adding visual information in play centers to help students get started
  - set out toys so they are ready to play, and
  - provide ideas.

TEACHING STUDENTS HOW TO USE PLAY SEQUENCES

Because we want our students to experience play with a variety of toys and to advance their skills through play, we teach organizational strategies to help them move from toy to toy during playtimes.

TEACH THE CONCEPT OF FIRST/NEXT

An important sequence that we make certain our children understand is first/next. Because this student finds first/next sequences meaningful, she accepts reading a book with her mother, not an activity she would choose. She knows next comes play with Froggy that makes a funny noise when dropped. Utilizing visual cues and consistently saying the same words, "First _____, next ______," we teach this concept across settings, so that children generalize the knowledge. Being successful in life means we delay what we prefer doing to complete a task first that we are expected to do. In addition to helping children try new toy activities, learning about first/next sequences is a valuable life lesson.

EMPHASIZE ALL DONE AND PUTTING AWAY

Learning to focus on one toy until finishing with it, putting it away, and then getting another eventually can help students manage playtimes independently and productively. This boy has a "start" basket filled with toys to play with on his left so that he knows where to find them and an "all done" basket on his right so that he knows where to put them when finished. He selects one toy, plays with it, and then puts it away in the all done basket before selecting another toy from the start basket. He can clearly see when he is all done because the start basket is empty. He tolerates trying new toys because the routine becomes so familiar, and he knows play with his favorite toy will be next.

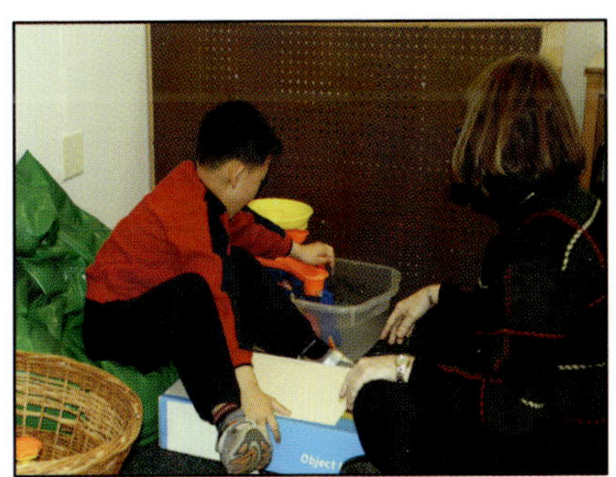    

ENCOURAGE STUDENTS TO USE PLAY SEQUENCES INDEPENDENTLY

After students learn to organize their toy play during one-to-one teaching times, they are ready to try similar toy sequences independently. Usually, our students will be more successful without teacher direction if they first practice using the organizational strategies in highly structured settings, such as this one, located in a quiet corner with a table and chair.

By looking on his table, the child has the answer about what toys. After playing with a toy placed in front of his chair, he places it in the finished basket to his right, and he then chooses any of the others. The student can tell when he is all done because all the toys are off of the table and in the finished basket. He knows that his favorite toy, in a container on the table, will be next. He takes his prized possession to an area where he can play as he wishes. Using the to-do list, first with his teacher and now independently, has taught him that toys are unique, have different purposes, and have starting and finishing points.

The student is now able to use his knowledge about how to play with toys in a more natural play setting. He quickly becomes engaged with the familiar racetrack because his teacher has set it out so that it is ready to play. As a result of the familiar organizational routine, he can sustain his attention with it until he finishes. He then knows to put the cars away and choose another toy. Limiting the number of toys and amount of space further enables him to manage his playtime independently.

ASSESSING STUDENTS' NEED FOR INDIVIDUAL PLAY SPACES

After teaching our students how to use new toys and play sequences and giving them time to practice these skills independently, we observe closely to see whether they will be able to generalize these strategies to more natural play spaces. We find there are students who continue to need a structured play corner for a variety of reasons. Some may be unable to attend well enough in a busy center to play productively, others may not move beyond their set play schemes, others may need some time in a quiet corner away from social demands so they can recharge their batteries before rejoining a group, and others may want to practice using new toys so they feel competent prior to playing with these toys with peers. We often use visual cues that help children know what toys they will play with, when they will be finished, and what they will do next. We pick the visual cues based on what the children find interesting or meaningful.

On his left, the student sees what toys he will play with first and what will be next, his beloved dinosaur. He plays with each until finished, puts the competed toy in a bin, and then gets to play as he wishes in an area with peers. The individual play space remains important for teaching this student to expand his toy play.

We never underestimate the power of children's interests and use these in many learning situations to capture their attention. Using an appealing theme eases this student into focusing on and using her play sequence. She willingly tries new toys when they are presented in this context, and she knows a favorite activity follows. She remains focused on her toy list even though her individual play space is in a play area with peers.

This student frequently plays with a variety of toys in play centers with peers, but he sometimes feels overwhelmed by the social demands. Having time to play with toys in a private space for a few minutes gives him a needed break before resuming play with his friends. Here, he chooses any three of the starred bins and completes the activity. When finished with the activity, he places it back in the bin and the bin back on the shelf. When he finishes with all three toys, he takes his name card to his schedule board to see what group activity he will join.

ENHANCING LEARNING THROUGH PLAY LISTS IN CLASSROOM CENTERS

Many classrooms are set up with play centers, and there are many students who can learn new skills within that context. For those students who are not advancing their play development in centers, we place play to-do lists that include novel activities and teach the organizational strategies of selecting a toy, using it appropriately until finished, putting it away, and getting another. We answer the questions about what toys to play with, when am I finished, and what do I do next by providing meaningful visual cues. To ensure that students know how to use the cues in a new setting, we directly teach there. After learning to use organizational strategies in play centers, we encourage students to manage their own playtimes.

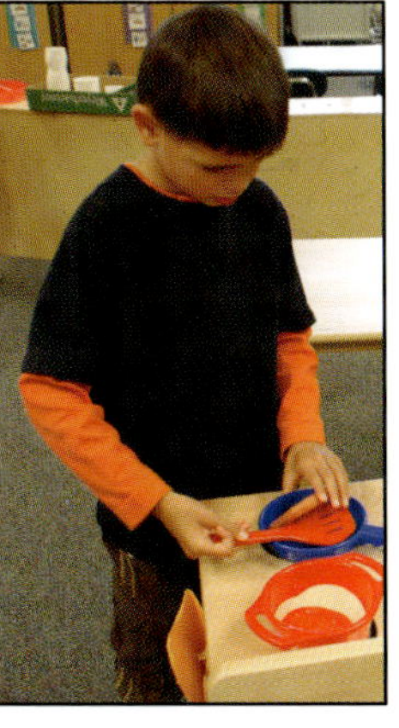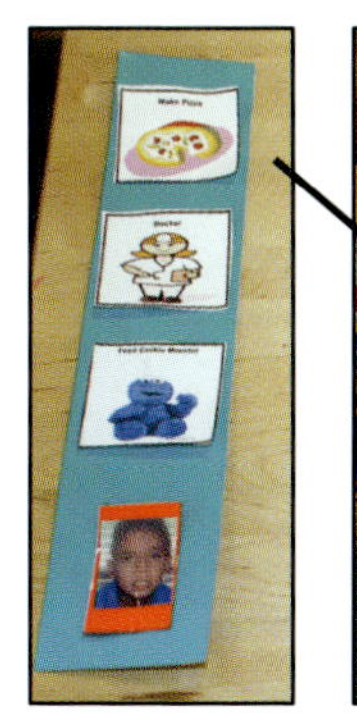

This child enjoyed center time and was ready to use toys symbolically. His repetitive themes, however, interfered with advancing his play skills. Here, his teacher provides a to-do list with matching pictures on the toy bins. The student sees he will make a pizza, play doctor, and feed Cookie Monster™. He takes each bin to a table, plays with the toys, and returns the toys to the bin and the bin to the shelf. He removes each picture from the list and places it in the bin with the toys after he completes each activity. When no pictures of toys remain on the list, he knows housekeeping play is all done, and he is to check his schedule. Through repeated practice, he knows to take his photo to his schedule board and see what activity follows.

This student now has a thorough knowledge of using sequences with a variety of toys. His teacher places play to-do lists in centers. The pictures and words on this list reveal the activities. Cards go in an "all done" pocket after he completes each one. Following his to-do list, he independently pretends to cook, eat, and wash dishes before choosing his favorite activity. Because the activities on his to-do list are similar to those of his classmates, the chances are greater that he and his peers will notice each other and play together.

HELPING STUDENTS GET STARTED IN A PLAY CENTER

Through teaching or instinct, some of our students manage their center playtimes fairly well. They attend to toys and learn new skills as they play. They sequence play steps and put away toys when finished. Often, what we find they still need strategies that help them get started with a toy because they may be overwhelmed by all the choices or stressed by social demands. Some simple additions to play centers, such as setting out toys so they are ready to play and providing ideas via visual prompts, can help with this conundrum.

SET OUT TOYS SO THEY ARE READY TO PLAY

Children arrive in a play center and see interesting and meaningful toys. Because it is not necessary for them to set these up, they are more likely to initiate play with them.

Finding the dinosaurs in a bin beside the mountain and toy tools and pegs beside a teacher-made work bench helps students quickly initiate play because they find toys whose purposes are clear. Also, not having to stop to figure out how to set up the toys helps the students engage.

When this teacher lays out ready to go toys, she often labels the bin with a photo of her student's playing with that toy. When the student sees her picture on this box in the play area, she initiates play with the zoo animals.

The tub is placed at the entrance to the housekeeping center, and the baby is ready for her bath. Also set out are the things the children will need for bathing, drying, and dressing baby. Prior setup means that the students spend less time arranging the bath and baby for play, and right away they play with each other. This is helpful because one of the students has a shorter attention span than the other and would lose interest in the activity if setting up the toy took too long. Getting to the fun play more quickly helps her stay engaged longer with her playmate.

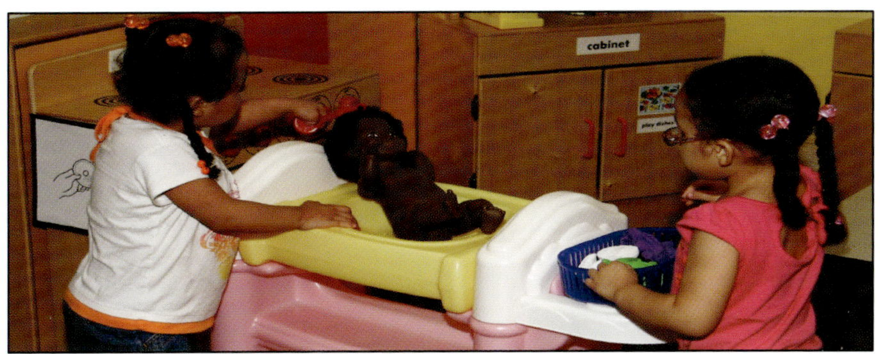

PROVIDE IDEAS

Sometimes students are able to initiate play if we give them ideas in the form of visual instructions. For some students, placing toys into bins so that pieces are separated and easy to find will be enough structure to help them pick a toy and start playing. For others, who still struggle to generate ideas, we place visual instructions that suggest possibilities into some of the bins. These can help some students initiate play because not having to think up an idea has made playing with the toy less stressful. By rotating types of toys or by offering several visual instructions for the

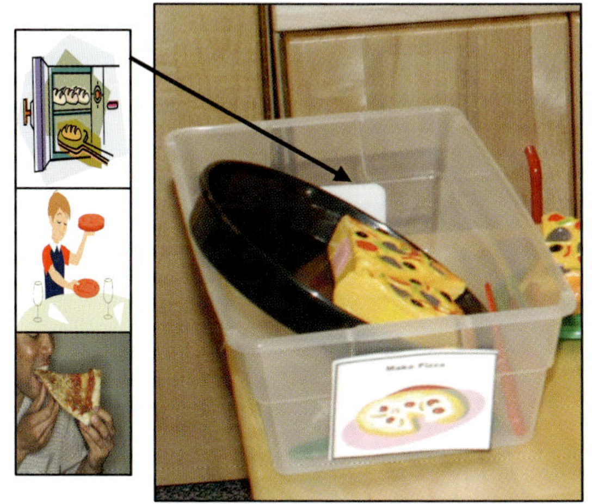

Sometimes we give our students a few suggestions to get them started with toys but then leave a blank space to encourage them to originate an idea. The blank visual prompt can be used in many different situations and become a reminder to students that this is a time to think independently and not rely on other's ideas.

This orange creature bends so it can be positioned in many different ways. The teacher provides two possibilities but leaves a blank card as a way of getting students to begin originating ideas about how to use new toys.

The theme in this classroom is types of weather. A student finds possibilities by a drawing board. The "I have an idea" and blank cards cue her to think of a different type of weather picture to draw.

One teacher talks with students during group times about the ideas of the day for different centers. When they go to those centers, they see reminders about the ideas. In the manipulative center, the idea for this day is to build a car out of bristle blocks. Once started with bristle blocks, the students often think of other things to build. In the housekeeping center, the teacher provides a suggested menu for the day. She also provides props for students to take orders from their playmates. Just seeing this idea when they enter the area is enough of a visual prompt for some to initiate play.

Students have prelearned play schemes, such as bathing baby, shopping, and cooking, and they feel confident playing with these toys with their peers. The books with visual instructions help the children remember the ideas and, if needed, give them something on which to focus. Students who manage their playtimes by choosing toys, attending to them until finished, putting them away, and choosing something different may sometimes have difficulty putting these skills in place when in a play center filled with commotion. These play books provide a starting point and help the children organize their thoughts about what to play when they are feeling overwhelmed in a center.

CHAPTER 4
MAKING CHOICES AND ENDING THEM

Children's play consists of making choices. They think about their options and, through choice-making, direct their activities. With ease, they pick what toy, how they want to play with it, and who they want to play with them. Because visualizing options, acting spontaneously, and thinking flexibly are not inherent skills for children with ASD and other developmental challenges, they have difficulty realizing their choices.   It is our responsibility as caregivers to make sure we instruct our children about choice-making skills. We begin this task by assessing whether students understand what making a choice means. Then we watch and see what toys and activities they choose spontaneously.   We notice whether they choose only what they can see or let someone know what they want when they cannot get it for themselves. We also pay attention to how they communicate their choices.

While playing, we want our students to know there are many possibilities, so they do not limit their choices to only those they know. Creating choice-making opportunities throughout our students' day means that it becomes routine for them to think about options. When this happens for our students, they are able to move beyond their rote recall of what they always play to considering more possibilities.

Playing with our choice always must end; we cannot play indefinitely. Many of our students resist putting away something they are really enjoying. They have difficulty shifting their focus from what they are doing to the next activity. Finish routines can make these potentially stressful times more tolerable.

To help students make choices and understand when those choices must end, consider
- ensuring that students understand what making a choice means,
- limiting choices,
- making choice-making part of daily routines
    - choose centers,
    - choose toys or activities, and
    - choose while playing with a toy,
- establishing routines for transitions from chosen activities
    - provide visual cues,
    - use anticipation countdowns,
    - clarify what comes next, and
    - set up procedures for finishing later.

ENSURING STUDENTS UNDERSTAND WHAT MAKING A CHOICE MEANS

Because of our eagerness to teach our students, we sometimes make the mistake of asking them to make choices among toys when they do not know how. We try to remember to assess whether they understand what making a choice means. We realize that the children do not know how to choose when they pick any object offered without showing a preference, attempt to choose all options, or do not attend to any of the toys.

We hope our students can learn what choice-making means by offering two options, one in which the child has no interest. If the children pick the toy of no interest, we guide them to look at each possibility again. Students often feel less stress if we make choosing more obvious. This mother offers her daughter either a peg or a truck as her choices; she knows her child has no interest in pegs. Her daughter looks at both, considers each, and then chooses the truck. Learning that communicating gets you something you really want increases the likelihood you might communicate more independently in future exchanges.

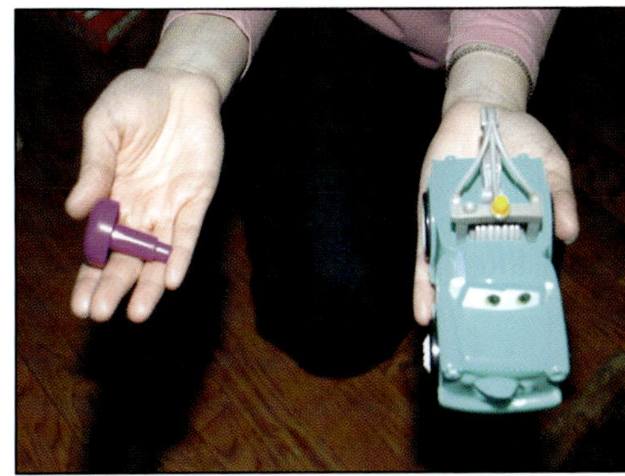

LIMITING CHOICES

When children first begin to make choices, we limit the options. If overwhelmed by too many, they may walk away without choosing anything.

Now that the mother knows her daughter understands what choice-making means, she offers a choice of only two cars so her daughter can more easily choose.

A teacher limits the number of options because her student cannot yet consider too many at once. Here, his two center choices are play or computer areas.

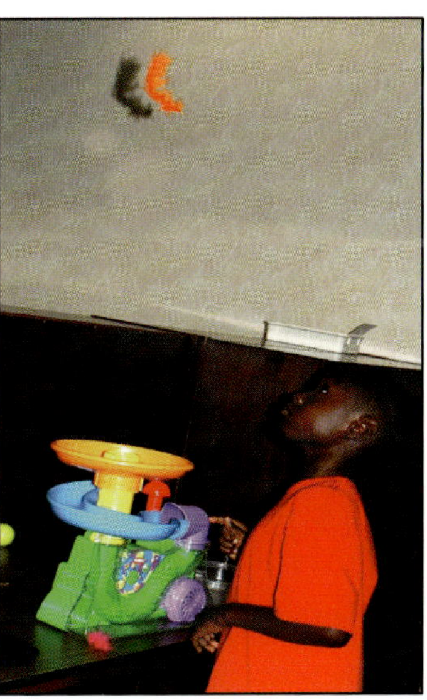

Head phones or feather represent two possible play choices for this student. He opts for a toy that blows the feather and lets his teacher know by taking the object to her.

MAKING CHOICE-MAKING PART OF DAILY ROUTINES

CHOOSE CENTERS

Most early learning settings utilize play centers, and frequently students can choose among these. We want our students to have the experience of choosing a center, and we also want them to play in a variety of centers. Children cannot make an informed choice about which center if they do not really understand what toys and activities are there. For example, the child who picks only the reading center will never know there are fun activities in the art, manipulative, and housekeeping centers as well. We limit or close centers occasionally so children will try them all.

Some students understand their center choices best if we represent those choices by objects. Here, the student chooses whether to take the book and go to the reading corner or the doll and go to the housekeeping center. Once there, she actually uses the objects.

The teacher limits the center choices to three (books, computer, or housekeeping), so her students can more easily scan them.

A card from this boy's individual daily schedule brings him to the center choice board. He places this card in the pocket at the top of the board.

After considering his three options, he selects one of the center cards. He will next go to that center where he will place the card in a pocket with a matching picture.

A teacher in an inclusive setting had her students pick both a center and a friend. At the end of group time, the teacher called students to come to where she was. There they saw their center choices and a visual reminder that first they were to choose a center and then choose a friend to play with them. The teacher gave students clips labeled with their names. They knew to match it to their center choice and then point out the chosen playmate. The children who were chosen by others and did not get to make their own choices knew from the routines that they would be the ones choosing next time. They also knew from the routines that the red, "X," on a center denoted that it was not a current choice and, if both orange spots were taken, that center was filled and, thus, not an option.

In some classrooms, the routine is for children to look around the classroom and find a center. Typically, however, there is a limit on how many children can play in a center at once. Here are examples of concrete visual cues we have used to help children with learning challenges recognize when a center is and is not available to them.

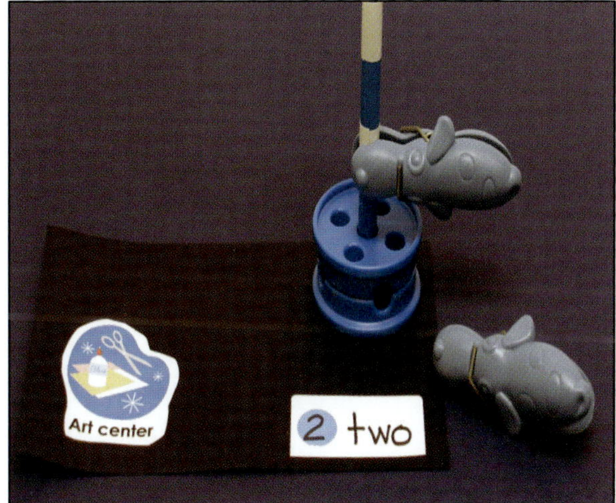

In the first example, the children take blocks with their pictures on them when looking for a center to choose. If the trays are filled, they recognize that the center is not open, and they will need to make another choice.

In the second example, students Velcro their names onto posters found at entries to centers. If there is no Velcro for their balloon, they know the center is not an option and to make a second choice.

At another school, the teacher placed Tinker Toy™ sticks with room for two clips at center entrances. Children check to see whether both spaces, identifiable by tape marks, are filled. If so, they look for a vacant center.

CHOOSE TOYS OR ACTIVITIES

Realizing there are choices and pausing to consider them are so important. Having many opportunities throughout the day for students to make choices among activities or toys gives good practice with choice-making. We often represent toy choices visually because we want to make sure our students realize there may sometimes be play possibilities even when they cannot see toys. We decide on which type of visual cue to represent choices based on what the individual student finds meaningful.

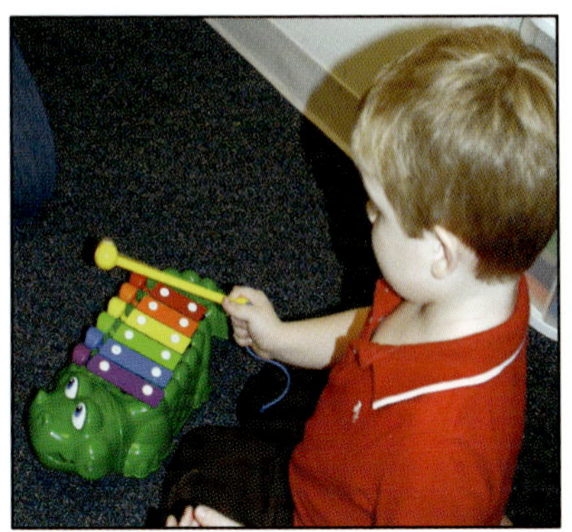

In this play center, there is a choice board with objects, representing toys, such as this mallet, which represents a xylophone. Through daily routine, her student learns to find the board with the options, think about which one he wants to play with, and then indicate that choice to his teacher. By needing his teacher to find the toy, he also initiates engagement with her.

Many of our students know how to follow individual or classroom schedules. When we offer them a board of possible choices, they may think this is just another schedule that tells them what they have to do instead of a board offering what is possible as choices.

We, thus, give thought to making choice boards look different from a linear left-to-right or top-to-bottom schedule. Here is a schedule from a kindergarten class in a typical top-to-bottom arrangement. These pictures indicate to the student what he must do. The options for toys and activities on the choice board, therefore, are arranged in a circular fashion, so students recognize it as different from a schedule.

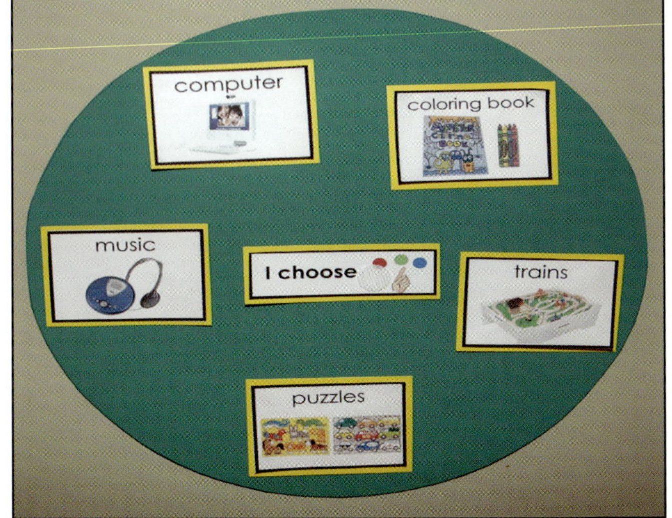

We frequently present toy or activity choices in pictures, written words, or both if we are certain our students find these meaningful.

A student is ready to see her choices on separate pages rather than all at once. We teach her to look at each page in the choose book thoughtfully and consider each option before making a selection.

A teacher wanted her student who loved Legos™ to know he could build all sorts of things with them. Here, she provides him with some options.

CHOOSE WHILE PLAYING WITH A TOY

We design toy activities so that students will practice choice-making in that context also. These different activities about faces provide opportunities for choosing. Students can select which glasses for Mr. Potato Head™ and whether to make him happy or sad. There are many funny looking eyes, noses, mouths, and tongues from which to choose to create Triangle Man.

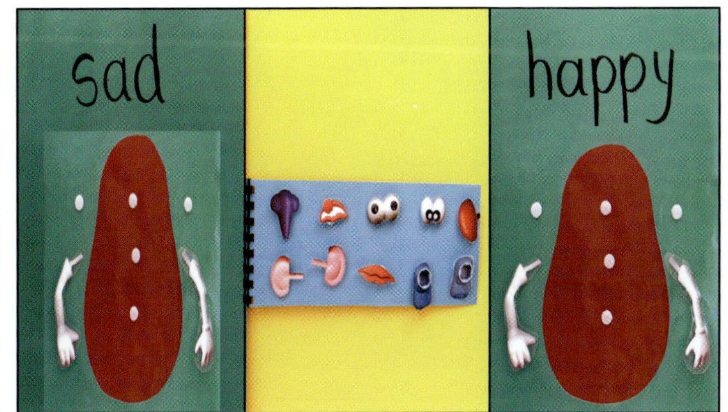

These students will choose which balloon they want to blow up. Their teacher takes the opportunity to teach how we sometimes use a pointing gesture combined with a look to let others know our choice.

Providing visual prompts encourages many of our students to use their language to make choices.

With a community helper play set, they can ask for a figure and then choose whether they want it to be short, tall, long, or short.

With their gears, they can choose to turn the toy off or on or have it go fast or slow.

The teacher provides possible choices of what the explorers do in the polar play set, so students can share their ideas.

ESTABLISHING ROUTINES FOR TRANSTIONS FROM CHOSEN ACTIVITIES

It is difficult to leave something you have chosen to do when you are not yet ready. Children with ASD can become so intensely focused on their choices, which may be their favorite activities, that shifting focus can be especially hard for them. We attempt to ease them into making transitions by establishing routines that are predictable. Transitions may become easier if we make them more predictable by providing visual cues, countdown systems, information about what is next, and assurances that incomplete activities can be finished later.

PROVIDE VISUAL CUES

Putting away a familiar and captivating toy can be really frustrating for any child but especially for the child with ASD who may find repeating the same action comforting. Refusing to put away a preferred toy or getting extremely upset when putting it away interferes with the development of play skills. Because we want to encourage our students to explore many different kinds of toys, we establish visually clear and consistent routines to help them predict when they must finish one activity to make a transition to the next.

One way to stress finishing is to have children put away materials they were using before they move to another activity. A bin placed in a play area gives them an easy way to put away toys when it is time to make a transition. By putting away, this student clearly recognizes balloon play is over and is a separate activity from the one he will do next.

This container with a finished card attached brought to the place where the children are playing may be an effective ending routine for many students. Children learn to put away their toys when they see this box and learn the meaning of this important word, finished.

When children begin to understand transitions, this goodbye box can become an appealing way to put away a favorite toy. When the children see the box, they know what is to happen. An accompanying song or rhyme, such as, "Goodbye (name of toy)," or "See you later, alligator," helps ease many students into a transition. For toys that are too large to put in a box, a goodbye sign, such as this one on a train table, can be used as the visual cue to indicate ending play.

USE ANTICIPATION COUNTDOWNS

A common practice is to give children advance notice when they must leave an activity. For children with ASD, we find adding visual cues makes our verbal notices more meaningful.

This countdown appeals to children with number interests. The caregiver shows the board when there are five minutes left for playtime. As each minute passes, the child is shown the board and reminded that there are four (then three, two, one) minutes until clean-up. Once learned, this countdown routine can be used in many different situations.

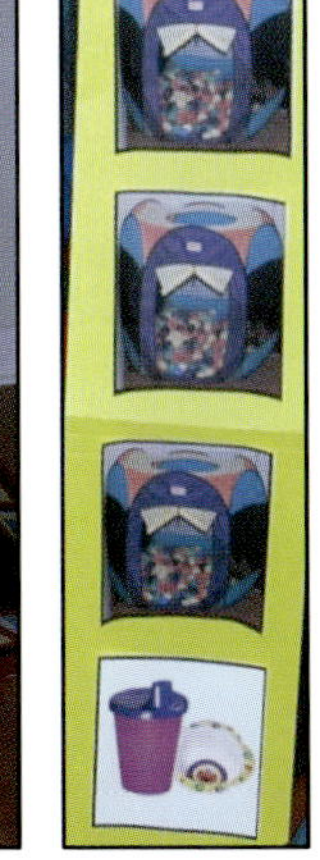

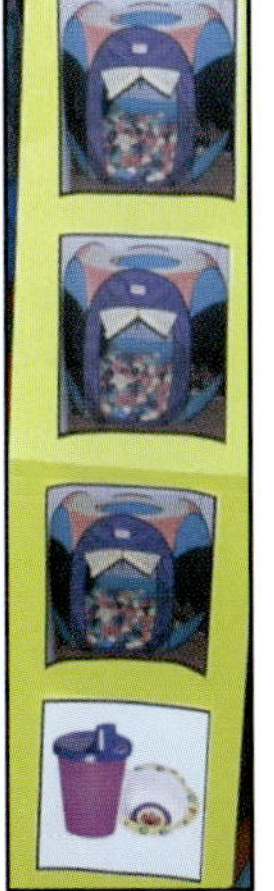

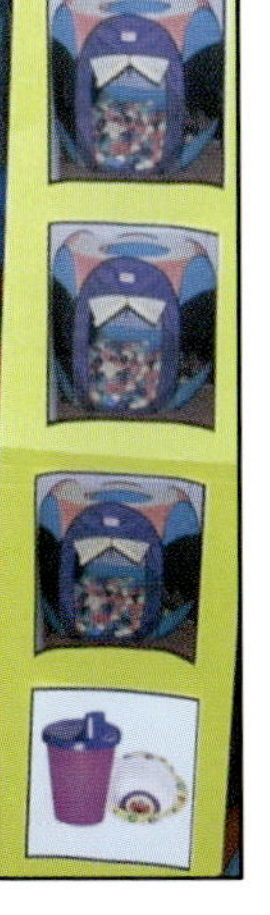

Fingers Velcroed down or "blast off" circles pulled off both visually show the countdown. Students often shift their attention to the appealing countdown systems and more readily leave one activity for the next. We try to find fun ways to use countdowns as well. Here, the students use the "blast off" system to countdown the balloon's send-off.

CLARIFY WHAT IS NEXT

It is even more beneficial to students with ASD if we incorporate into our visual countdown systems an indicator of what is next. We more willingly leave our preferred choice if we know what will happen next.

A common parenting practice is to give children advance notice when they must leave one activity. This mother uses three photos of the ball pit. She shows her child the board with these and says, "It is almost time to finish balls and get a drink" (the next activity) and removes the first photo. After all the ball pit pictures are removed, the child has the visual reminder of drink, so he remembers what is next. Preparing children for transitions by giving them advance notice and letting them know what is next creates less frustration.

For children who love stop lights, we use this type of countdown system with a what's next reminder. This, too, interrupts the child, but in a fun way. When the children see their teacher bringing the stoplight board to them, they know they must stop what they are doing after hearing, "Red, yellow, green, go to music." Enthusiasm, songs, or rhymes can be added to make even transitions interesting.

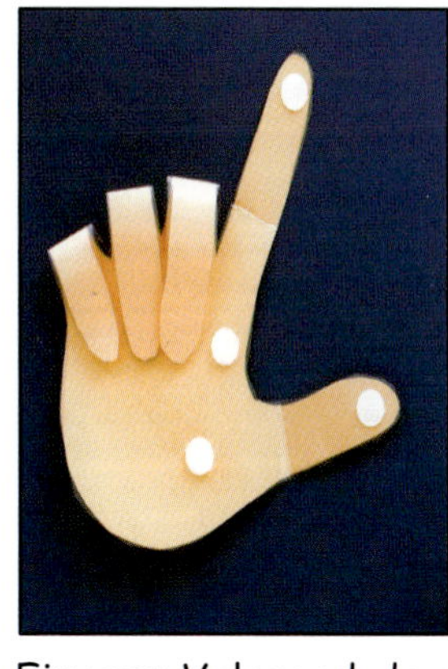

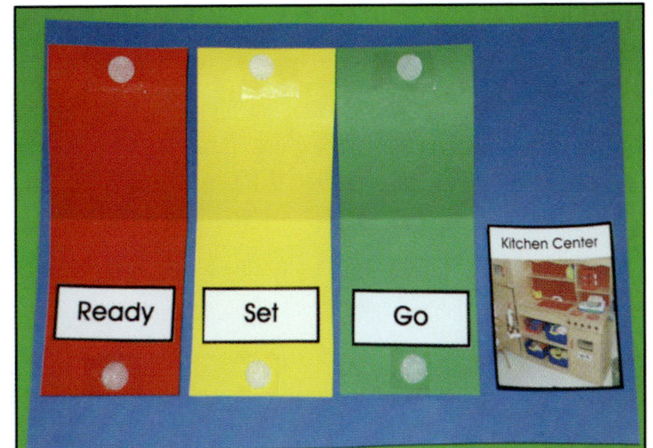

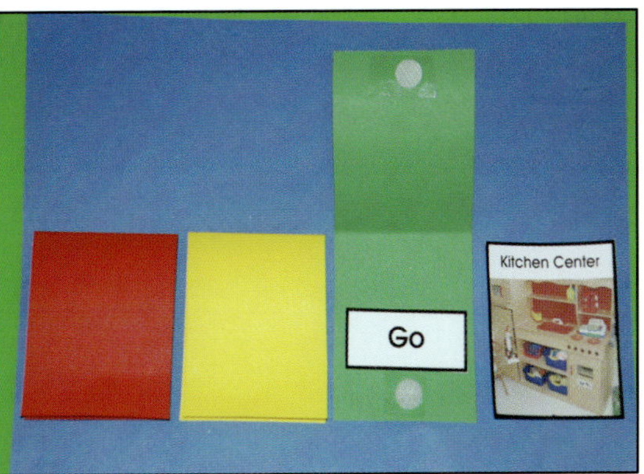

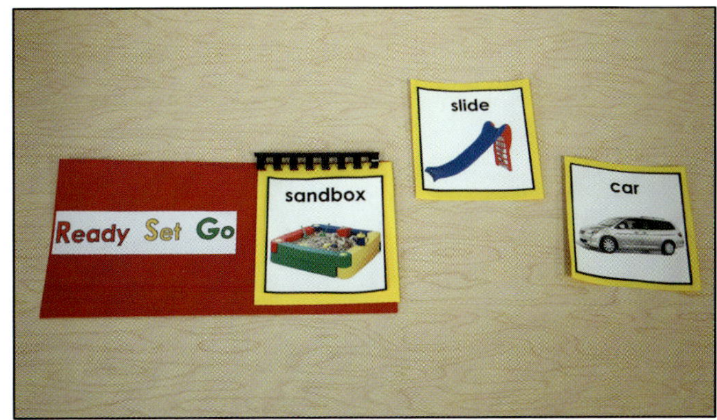

Another technique that has been used successfully with other children is incorporating the familiar "Ready, Set, Go" phrase into a finish routine. A teacher used this ready, set, go routine in her classroom. When it is time for her student to make a transition, she brings this board to her and says in a most enthusiastic manner, "Samantha, ready, set, go!" The teacher engages her student in the process by having her cover the words with the flaps. Sometimes this becomes a fun interruption and makes the transition more tolerable. The student now sees only the uncovered picture that remains, which depicts what is next. In this case, next is to go to the kitchen center.

Routinely practiced in her classroom, the student's parent uses the ready, set, go visual at the playground. As a result, the child makes easier transitions among equipment and tries new activities. When it is time to leave, her mother shows the ready, set, go book with the picture of her car clarifying what is next. Because her daughter had learned this routine so well, she is much more willing to leave the playground.

SET UP PROCEDURES FOR FINISHING LATER

Some children ease into a transition better if they know they can finish later.

This teacher provides "Finish later; I'll be back" signs that students can place on activities that they have not completed. Through routine, they learn that their activity has been undisturbed once they return to it. They are more able to focus on other activities because they see a card on their daily schedules that lets them know when they will return to their project so they can complete it.

CHAPTER 5
IT'S PRETEND

Playing is essential to a child's cognitive development; therefore, giving our students the tools to play symbolically is essential. Many of our students may appear to imagine. If we look more closely, however, we realize that they are more adept at memorizing play scenarios and at using prompts than at thinking creatively and spontaneously. The cognitive differences identified in individuals with ASD have bearing on the development of pretend play, just as they have bearing on academic learning. These differences express themselves in the difficulties our students have generalizing knowledge, organizing steps, integrating ideas, and thinking abstractly. We use these differences as our roadmap when attempting to teach underlying concepts that someday can enhance creativity both in their pretend world of play and in their real world of school and life tasks.

To help our students pretend, consider teaching students how to

generalize what they already know
- from using objects,
- from watching others, and
- from information in books and DVD's,

organize individual play ideas into a logical sequence,

integrate concepts into play
- general associations,
- associations about what belongs together,
- cause and effect relationships,
- sounds or words conventionally used,
- emotions, and
- classroom themes,

think abstractly
- make dolls act,
- be silly and absurd,
- pretend an object is something else,
- pretend an object is really there, and
- pretend to be someone else,

originate thoughts
- use different toys for the same purpose,
- make choices,
- change sequence or script,
- include something hand-made into pretend play, and
- think of new ideas.

GENERALIZING EXPERIENCES TO SYMBOLIC PLAY

Many play ideas derive from our life experiences. Objects children use and actions they take provide starting ideas for pretend play. Young children also gain many notions about what to pretend from watching their caregivers. We try to help our students become more aware of others' daily actions and show how to pretend these. Characters offer more ideas as children pretend what they saw while watching DVDs or listening to stories. Our task as educators is to be aware of what our students find meaningful in their everyday experiences and then provide props and visual supports to help them act out this real-world knowledge symbolically.

FAMILIAR OBJECTS AND ACTIONS

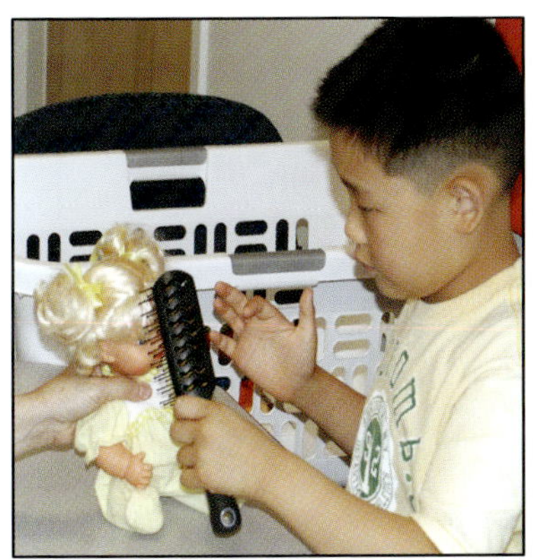

He learns to brush his hair and then the doll's hair.

He puts on the sunglasses, and now Teddy has on sunglasses.

Other early ideas for pretense come from everyday actions that children do, such as eating and drinking. Instead of actually drinking, this child understands how to pretend to drink or symbolize drinking. He then extends this action to others and, thereby, generalizes his knowledge about drinking into his play.

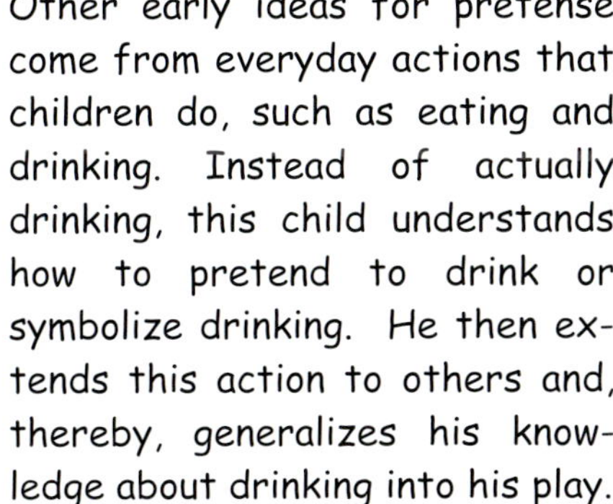

He pretends to drink.

He gives his teacher a pretend drink.

Puppet gets a pretend drink.

KNOWLEDGE LEARNED FROM WATCHING OTHERS

Watching what grown-ups do in real life gives more ideas for make-believe. This child pretends to talk on his toy phone as he sees his teacher do on her real phone. Another student knows about driving cars from watching his parents. He generalizes this knowledge when he makes believe that he drives his toy car.

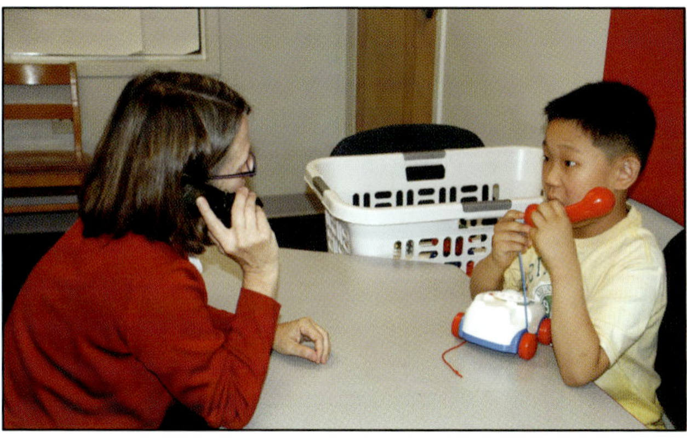

KNOWLEDGE LEARNED FROM BOOKS OR DVDs

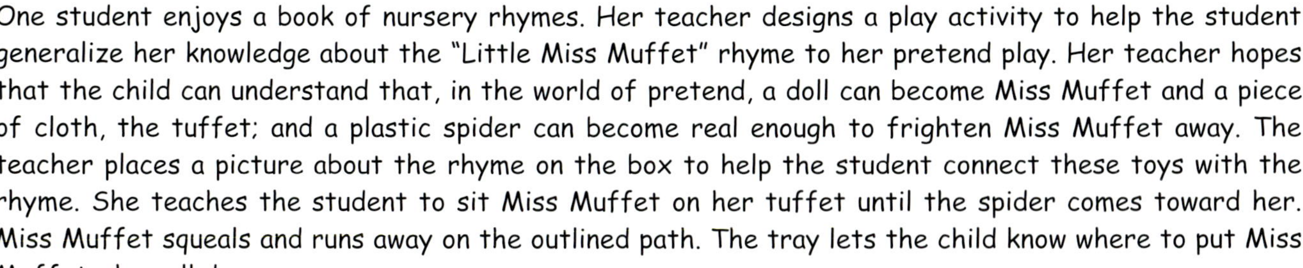

One student enjoys a book of nursery rhymes. Her teacher designs a play activity to help the student generalize her knowledge about the "Little Miss Muffet" rhyme to her pretend play. Her teacher hopes that the child can understand that, in the world of pretend, a doll can become Miss Muffet and a piece of cloth, the tuffet; and a plastic spider can become real enough to frighten Miss Muffet away. The teacher places a picture about the rhyme on the box to help the student connect these toys with the rhyme. She teaches the student to sit Miss Muffet on her tuffet until the spider comes toward her. Miss Muffet squeals and runs away on the outlined path. The tray lets the child know where to put Miss Muffet when all done.

Spiderman characters climb up the side of one "building" and swing about before disappearing into another "building." This student is familiar with these actions from watching Spiderman cartoons. His teacher provides him with the props to act out the action he has seen and finds meaningful. He is able to generalize his knowledge about the cartoon character to his pretend play.

SEQUENCING IDEAS

As children mature, their play becomes more complex. They integrate different types of toys and different types of actions into logically themed sequences. Developing coordinated individual ideas into step-by-step play is quite difficult for children with developmental problems. Using visual strategies, we might begin by teaching students to add a pretend step to a functional play sequence.

Here, we take the familiar, everyday activity of eating. First, the student follows directions that outline the steps of making a pizza: make the crust, then add cheese, then pepperoni, followed by peppers. When she finishes assembling her felt pizza, the last picture reminds her to pretend to eat it. What could have been just a manipulative task, thus, becomes a symbolic one.

We also help students develop play scripts or sequences by teaching them what someone or something might do. We teach the steps individually and then show students how they can put the ideas together for play scripts. Here, students learn what dogs might do. Developing a conceptual understanding about dogs: they are animals; they say, "Woof;" they eat bones; they sleep in doghouses, etc.; helps the children better understand the world in general and become more aware of dogs in their environment. This teacher helps her students use toys to act out ideas about dogs. She first teaches the individual steps of how a toy dog goes into a dog house and, next, how to pretend the toy dog eats a bone. She then shows students how to put these ideas into a two-step sequence: dog stops to eat the bone in his path before going into the doghouse. Here, several dogs line up for a turn. The student gets repeated practice with the sequence and can determine how long the activity will last - until all dogs are in the doghouse.

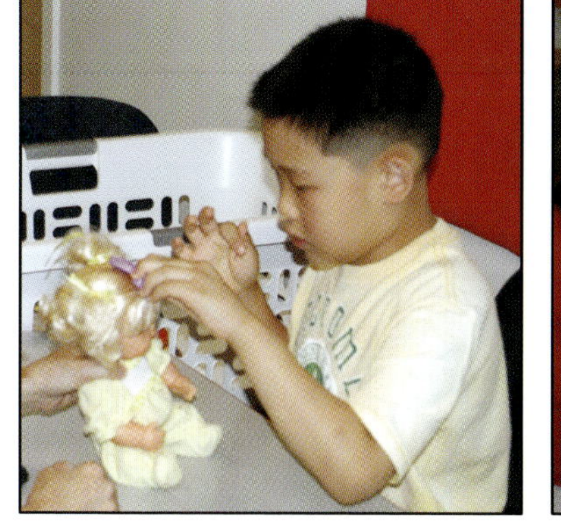 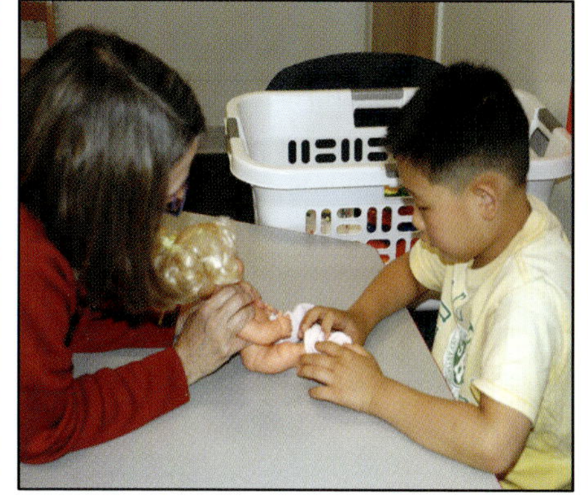 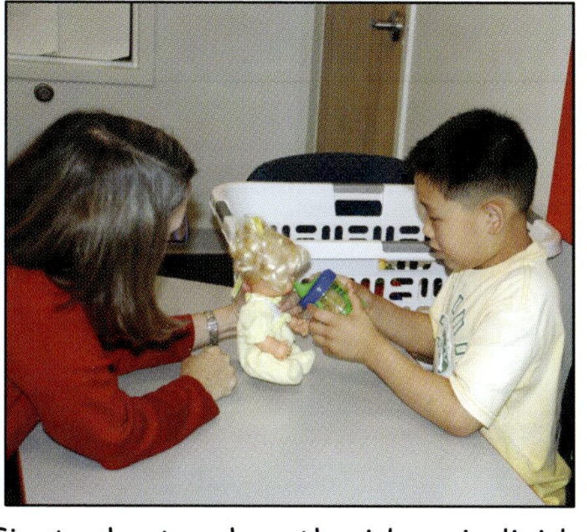 

Here, a teacher instructs her student what babies might require. First, she teaches the ideas individually and, then, places possible props in a bin to encourage sequencing the ideas. For some students, she displays a series of pictures to show the possibilities and sequence.

 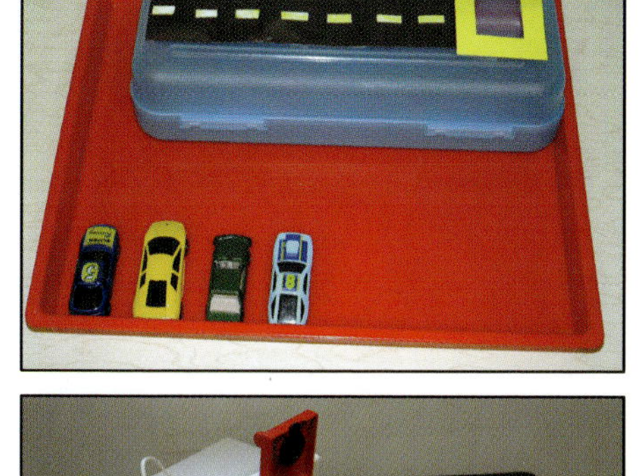  

In this example, we design structured individual play activities to show what cars can do: ride on a road, go through a car wash, and park in a garage. We often teach these play activities during one-to-one teaching sessions and, then, help students understand how these individual activities can be combined into a themed play sequence about vehicles. When we first ask students to combine individual activities into a sequence, we include the same or similar toys used when teaching individual steps.

Real-life adventures more easily become play scripts and sequences when we provide pictured steps.

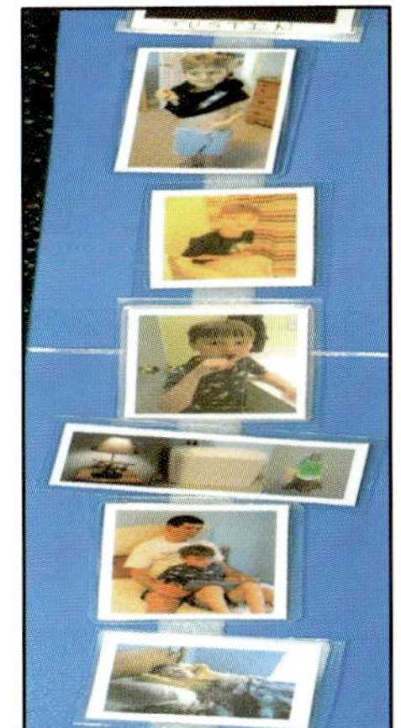

This teacher helps her student connect the bedtime routine pictures that he uses every night at home to doll house play. With encouragement, he acts out the sequence using a doll house, furnishings, and figures. Here, he pretends that the daddy doll reads a story to the boy doll, just as in real life, his daddy reads him a book.

Another child's mother takes photos of her son during a grocery store outing. She organizes these into a book and reads the story to her son. Next, she provides props: toy shopping cart, cash register, and real food items, and shows the photos to remind her son what he did at the grocery store. These sequenced photos become his play script for acting out grocery shopping.

Similarly, drawings remind this youngster what happens at doctor visits. Seeing the drawings supports his acting the steps symbolically. Because many of our students enjoy numbers, numbered sequences are both interesting and understandable formats for play scripts.

INTEGRATING ASSOCIATIVE RELATIONSHIPS

As children's minds expand, they understand more and more about associative relationships. By acting these out in their play, they strengthen their conceptual understanding. Typically while playing, children make general and specific associations; realize how one event links to another; connect language, sounds, and feelings to play activities; and figure out how to act out classroom themes.

GENERAL ASSOCIATIONS

Before symbolic play develops, young children begin to make general associations as they explore. For example, they learn that all sorts of objects open and shut: real doors, doors on toy trucks, etc. Experimenting with what opens and what closes leads to one of the first conceptual associations. Soon, children learn that objects can go into things. At this exploration stage, they may not yet have an understanding of what objects belong together, such as people ride in cars, or trash goes in garbage trucks. They do, however, develop the general association of how things go into other things. Now that the door is open, this child experiments with what will fit into his toy truck.

When children do not naturally play by putting objects in and taking them out, we might set up activities that have put-in components. One child understands putting in objects when playing with toys specifically designed for that purpose, such as this truck with slits for shapes. The teacher highlights the openings to increase the student's focus and lays the blue and yellow shapes on the play mat. To help students advance to a general association about putting in, we might ask them to put other kinds of objects into this truck or put these shapes into a different type of vehicle.

ASSOCIATIONS ABOUT WHAT BELONGS TOGETHER

Our students may demonstrate knowledge about what goes together with preschool games and worksheets, yet we notice that they do not include this conceptual understanding while playing. They often apply knowledge rotely or in the way they first learned it. If we can help them use this information in new and symbolic ways, we help them think more flexibly.

Sometimes, we teach students to make connections between real objects that go together before we ask them to imagine. This student really pours water into cups.

A shoebox task helps another student make associations between a hammer and pegs. Later the student sees a hammer, pegs, and Styrofoam set up as a play center activity. Because he knows what goes together and can use this knowledge flexibly, he is able to pretend he is hammering nails in this new setting with different materials.

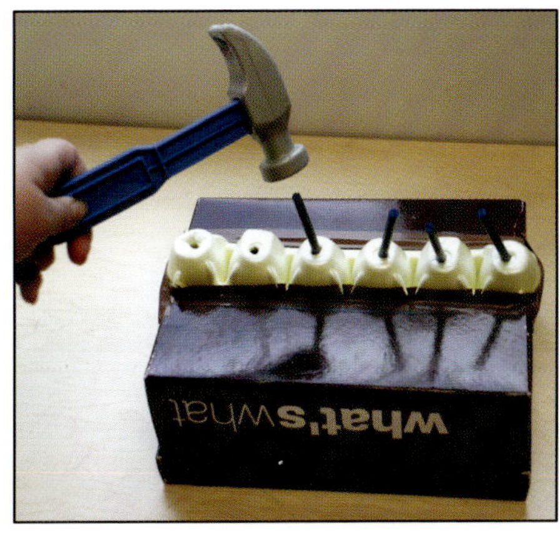

Some children may associate toy figures with this bus only because they fit into openings; the students insert the figures as they would insert puzzle pieces. They combine two objects correctly but without conceptually understanding that children belong in school buses.

Another child may realize that toy figures can ride in toy cars but makes the association only when the character is specific, such as this Spiderman, and the car is specific, such as this Spiderman car. The association is based on very specific criteria and not a universal association. When students, however, realize that any toy figure can ride in any toy vehicle, they have a firmer understanding of the connection between people and transportation and can more readily use this concept symbolically and flexibly while playing.

RELATIONSHIPS AND CAUSALITY

Through experiences, children begin to understand how one event occurs and then another usually follows. There is causality in these relationships. Children pretend many linked sequences when they develop this conceptual understanding.

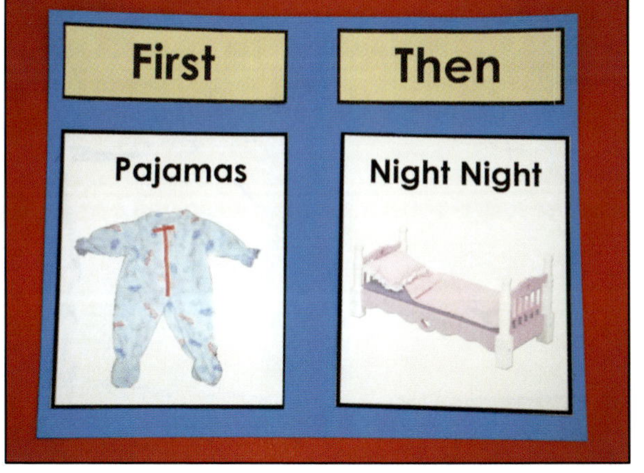

One cause-and-effect relationship that children enjoy pretending is using a band aid. A typical script may be that doggie falls down, hurts his back, and needs a band aid.

With these pictures, we help students understand the relationship between what the doll wears and what she does next. Children dress their doll in her shirt and shorts and then take her to the park, or they dress the doll in her pajamas and then put her to bed. Children begin to understand that what the doll wears has a relationship to what she does next.

One teacher used these day and night scenes to help her students connect different activities to time of day. If it is daytime, it is time for Teddy to ride the school bus, go to school, or read a book. If it is nighttime, it is time for Teddy to get his blanket, pillow, and little Teddy Bear and go to bed. We teach these events and resulting sequences during one-to-one teaching sessions and eventually provide the toys and visual reminders during center times to help students act out the associations independently.

Students' play advances when they make connections between what babies pretend to do and what is to happen next. Here, the student sees a picture of a yawning baby, which tells her what baby is doing. The next picture tells her what she, as the pretend mother, should do next, rock baby.

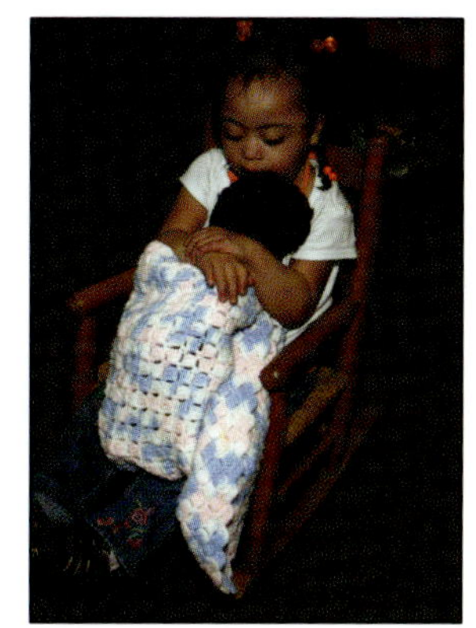

After reading a story about tow trucks, this teacher develops scripts for the car and tow truck drivers. Picture scripts include ideas about how one event results in the next: car needs gas and goes to the gas station or car hits a tree, and the driver calls for a tow truck.

The student hears the story about a tow truck.

Teacher develops scripts for the car and tow truck.

The car crashes into an apple tree.

The student refers to her car driver script to see what happens next.

She tows her crashed car to the garage.

ASSOCIATE SOUNDS AND WORDS

Most young children spontaneously use sounds and language with particular toys. If our students do not make these associations, we help them pair conventional sounds and words with toys and actions. For some children these adopted words turn into a monologue that guides their pretense or words that encourage their peers to join them.

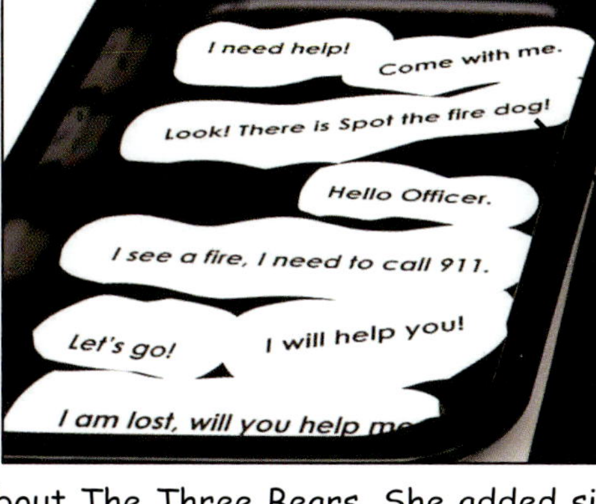

By exaggerating the sound and then pausing, this teacher encourages her student to copy a "Yum, yum" sound when he gives the puppet a bite. We find this is a good beginning sound for teaching students to associate language to a play activity.

Another student learns sounds and words that accompany car play. While driving a car mounted on a string affixed to a shoebox lid, his teacher indicates with drawings possible sounds or words. By using the visual cues, the student can recall more independently the sounds and be less dependent on copying teacher prompts.

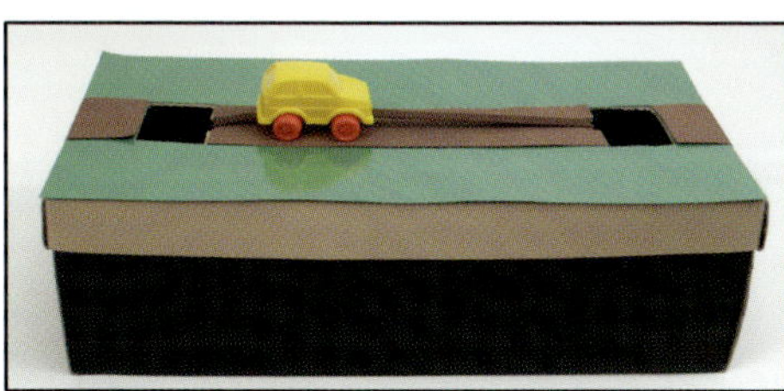

One teacher provided props for acting out the story about The Three Bears. She added simple sentences from the story. These cued students, even some who could not yet read, to use words the bears used. We find having students act out scenes from books with repetitive lines helps them associate the language when pretending. In firehouse play with toy figures, students can choose cards that suggest what their character might say. They then pretend that their character says the words while acting out the scenario.

ASSOCIATE EMOTIONS

Places where children play are seldom quiet. Sounds fill the air as children express their emotions freely. Many of our students need us to teach them the facial expressions and body language to associate with emotions. We often create activities for teaching our students to match their facial expressions to emotions. This student, assisted by the teacher's modeling and pictures, pretends to be scared, mad, surprised, or happy. Looking in the mirror creates more interest and helps her see the changes in her face.

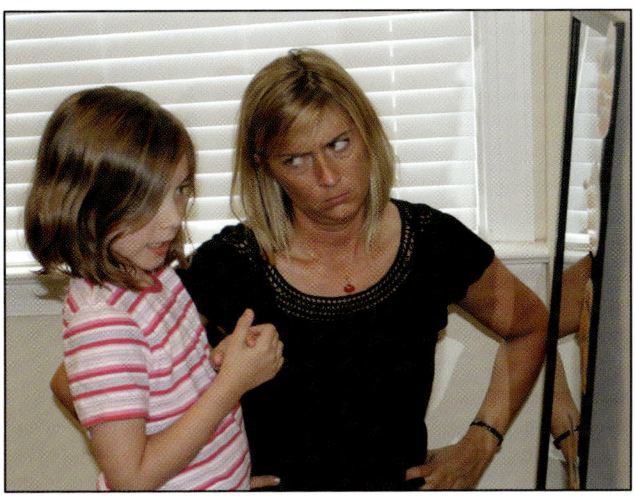

These students go on an emotions scavenger hunt. Their teacher gives them a card with the emotion pictures they are to find. When the students locate an emotion picture, their teacher points out changes in the facial expression. The teacher then acts out the emotion. Here, she hands students tissues so they can pretend to be sad also. After each student pretends to be sad, happy, mad, or shocked by something yucky, he removes the face with that emotion from his card. When the children remove all the cards, they have pretended each emotion and know the game is over.

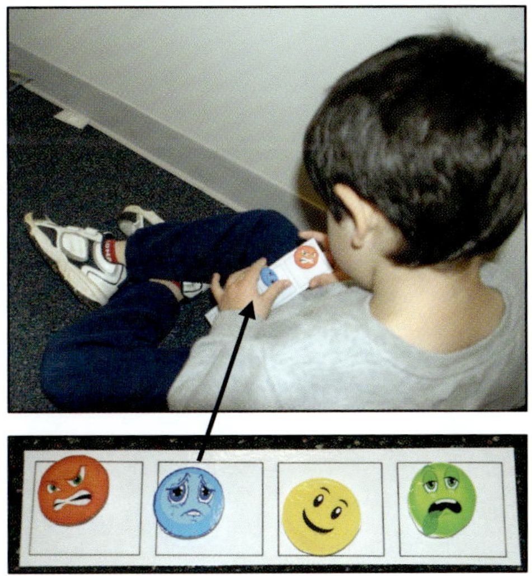

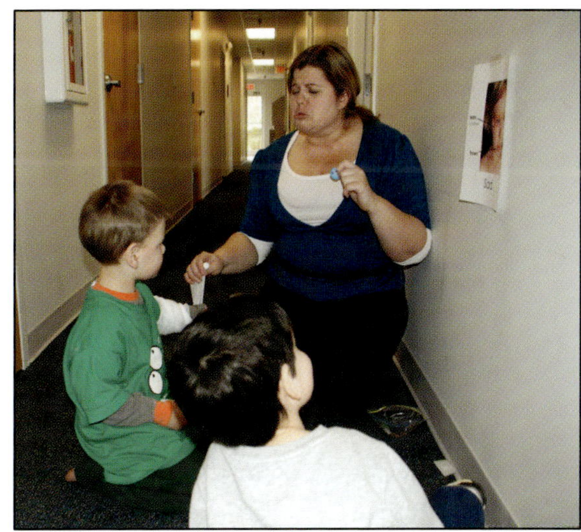

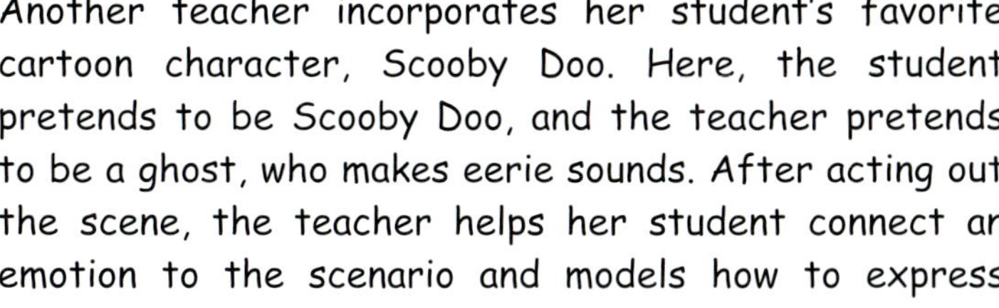

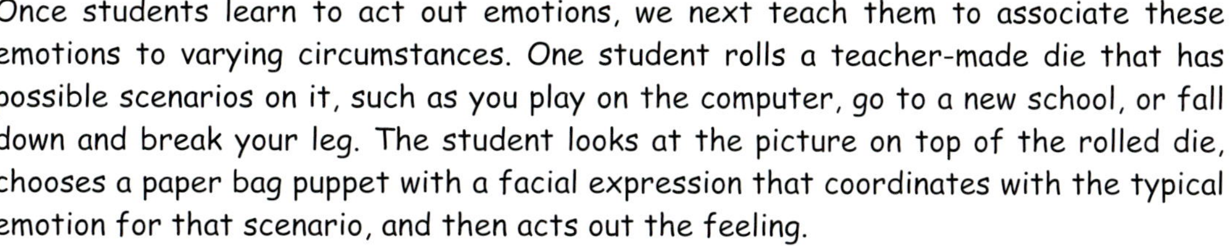

Once students learn to act out emotions, we next teach them to associate these emotions to varying circumstances. One student rolls a teacher-made die that has possible scenarios on it, such as you play on the computer, go to a new school, or fall down and break your leg. The student looks at the picture on top of the rolled die, chooses a paper bag puppet with a facial expression that coordinates with the typical emotion for that scenario, and then acts out the feeling.

Another teacher incorporates her student's favorite cartoon character, Scooby Doo. Here, the student pretends to be Scooby Doo, and the teacher pretends to be a ghost, who makes eerie sounds. After acting out the scene, the teacher helps her student connect an emotion to the scenario and models how to express being scared.

We also try teaching students how to respond to others' emotions during their symbolic play. These visuals help students associate their response with a baby's emotion. The red circle has a picture of a happy baby attached to the moveable arrow and the green circle has a picture of a crying baby. The pictures that surround the happy or crying baby are possibilities of what mothers or fathers do when their baby expresses one of these emotions. For a happy baby, the student can pretend to play peek-a-boo, take a walk, read a book, swing high, play this little piggy, or give a tickle to make the baby feel happy. To help a crying baby, the pretend daddy might rock the baby, put the baby to bed, give a pacifier or bottle, change a diaper, or put on a band aid.

ASSOCIATE CLASSROOM THEMES

Most early childhood curricula are organized around classroom themes. It is essential that we give children with developmental challenges opportunities to act out aspects of these themes symbolically. In this classroom, the theme for the month is farm animals. The teacher individualizes to ensure pretend farm activities are at each child's play level.

This student pretends to put each animal into the barn.

This student understands having his animal walk on the path to the barn.

Another child picks a card from the blue bin which has suggestions in pictures and words about what animals and the farmer can do.

This is an example of an activity to use with students at different play levels. One child may find animals in the corn and place them on their match, while a playmate pretends to be a farmer who tells the animals to run through the corn.

One student follows steps to make a pig and then sees steps that guide him to pretend with his hand-made creation. Here, his pig plays with a toy horse.

THINKING ABSTRACTLY

As children develop, they begin to think beyond the concrete and customary toy usage and become more and more creative in what they pretend. Their ideas sometimes forego reality, so that, in their minds, toys can act, an object can substitute for something other than what it really is, and they can become someone other than themselves. Because these types of play ideas may not occur naturally for children with learning challenges, we design activities in an attempt to guide them to think in this less literal manner.

PRETEND A TOY CAN ACT

Having the doll or toy figure carry out or become the agent of some action is not something that many children with ASD consider in their play. They may become quite experienced with using toys for pretense, but they remain the actor or the agent of the action. When the doll becomes the agent of the action, the child becomes the director of the scene and decides what characters will do. In this photo, two children use toy vacuums differently in their play. One student remains the actor as he uses the vacuum on the toy table; the other student fits the toy vacuum into the hand of his Daddy toy. He will have Daddy pretend to vacuum; his toy becomes the actor.

We first attempt to teach students to understand how an inanimate toy can act by having them pretend that a toy can carry out an action that the students often do. Here, the student makes the hand of his toy Elmo™ push the ball down a chute just as the student has done many times before while using his own hand. Another strategy we use is laying out a path. Here, a drawn path reinforces the idea of having his toy people walk to the boat instead of his just putting them inside of it.

There is vacuuming to be done, and three family members take turns. Placing the characters in chairs while they wait for their turn, and having picture cues showing each character using the vacuum can make this abstract pretend play more meaningful for many students.

The cow does many activities at her farm: she drinks water, walks on the path, eats hay in the barn, and goes inside the corral. Once children understand they are to pretend the cow does these actions, we next help them understand that other animals can do the same actions.

One teacher structured play with the doll house to encourage her students to have toy figures carry out the action. By having the students pick a toy figure from the "Who Bin" and an object from the "What Bin," they start to understand better the connections among characters, objects, and actions.

LEARN WHAT IS SILLY AND ABSURD

Children with ASD are sometimes adamant about dealing only with real-life situations. This mindset does not leave room for imagination. They cannot comprehend how a pretend doll could eat, or how they could pretend to be a mother. For these students, it may help to teach what silly means. Within the context of structured tasks, we try to encourage our students to consider absurd situations and model how funny absurdities can be. As a result, some students previously with rigid points of view can develop their senses of humor and be more willing to entertain possibilities for abstractions.

One teacher created a book to distinguish what is real versus what is silly. For each page, she provided a cutout of either a real or silly association. Her student first made the accurate, real-life connection, such as a duck goes into the water. On the next page, the teacher provided a bed, not a pond as the place for the duck. She helped her student attach the duck to the bed, showed a visual reminder about silly, and laughed enthusiastically about how silly it was for a duck to sleep on a bed. Once students willingly make silly associations, we might encourage them to show something that is pretend, not real, but silly with toys: an alligator drinking a soda; a man talking on a banana; those are so silly!

Another teacher incorporates some of the student's favorite characters. Instead of the student's doing the expected action for that character, however, his teacher guides him to pick *Who?* and *Is Doing?* from the picture cards provided. The teacher and child take turns, so she can model how funny absurdities can be and guide his thinking away from how horrible it is to have Thomas or Shrek do something out of character or unrealistic. Becoming comfortable with absurdities is a beginning step for students to play more creatively.

PRETEND AN OBJECT IS SOMETHING ELSE

After our students recognize, accept, and, hopefully, enjoy absurd situations, we introduce simple absurdities into their play with toys. We introduce ideas to guide their thoughts beyond the actual properties of an object and its conventional use. They begin to imagine that an object can represent or substitute for something else. Often switching to less realistic-looking toys begins when children have an idea but do not have the typical prop. They begin to think, "I want to hammer. I don't have a hammer. What could be a hammer?" Children with ASD tend not to think beyond the literal and concrete; they probably would not search out other possibilities for a hammer if a toy one were not available. If they have accomplished prior levels of symbolic play, however, we next guide them to see how a less realistic-looking object can substitute. If they can begin to think in these ways, groundwork will be laid to help them think more flexibly when it comes to future life and school tasks.

We suggest they substitute a less realistic-looking object when the students understand well the meaning of some object and its function. This student already pretends to feed stuffed animals or dolls realistic-looking plastic foods, such as a banana or an apple. His teacher suggests that he use a nonliteral object, a Lincoln Log™, as the pretend food. She makes the familiar "Yum, yum" sound as an additional way for the child to understand that the Lincoln Log™ may not look like food but, in a pretend world, may become food.

Pictures in a teacher-made Bob the Builder™ book depict different tasks Bob might do, such as hammer, saw, and measure. A student, who takes delight in this character first learns how to use realistic-looking toy tools to pretend these tasks. Then the teacher inserts new pages into the book to show how the student can substitute less representational objects to measure a block with a string, hammer a peg with a stick, and saw a piece of wood with a Lego™. In this example, after the child learns to measure a block with a toy tape measure, he sees a new picture in his book that suggests he measure the block with a string, a substitute that has similar properties to a tape measure.

After our student has many skating experiences at the rink, we know he understands about skating. We show him these funny shoebox skates, put them on our feet, and pretend to skate. We encourage our student to pretend that he is skating, too. For children who need additional help understanding how shoeboxes could become skates, we add pictures of skates to the front of the boxes. If these types of substitutions become comprehensible to our students, we may suggest an idea and have them look around for something they could use to act it out. Children frequently find household objects to be good substitutes in their pretend worlds.

Singing "The Wheels on the Bus" helps some students connect this line of chairs and a plate steering wheel symbolically to a real bus.

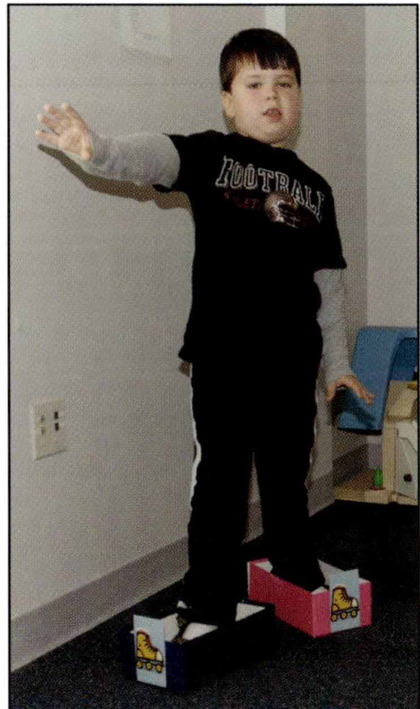

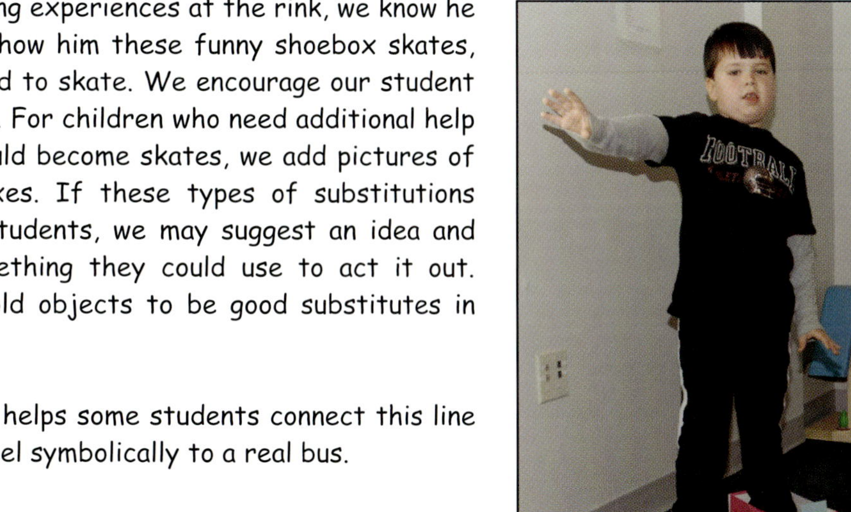

This telephone play represents a sequence we might go through to help students understand how one object can become another symbolically. First, the students play with realistic telephones; next, they use cups with pipe cleaner cords so that the object used to stand for a telephone shares a few characteristics with a phone. Finally, into a bin labeled, "I have an idea," the teacher places several objects that share little likeness to a phone. She guides her students to choose one, such as this blue foam pig, and pretend on talk on it as if it were really a phone. She incorporates the previously taught idea about absurdities and models how much she enjoys things that are silly.

PRETEND AN OBJECT IS THERE

Frequently young children wish to pretend, do not have a realistic object to use, and do not take the time to find a substitute. Yet they still pretend the action but without any object. For example, they pretend to drink but do not use a cup or a substitute. They pose their hand into a cup and pretend to take a drink. This is another hard step for literal and visual thinkers. How can nothing become something? We ask children to try out this play step if they have succeeded with earlier abstract ones.

During a Simon Says or Follow the Leader game, this student's teacher gives simple directions quickly. Sometimes, the teacher provides toy props for the child to use; sometimes, she gives the same direction but does not provide the prop. Once into the rhythm of the game, this student automatically used his hands to pretend to eat when no toy watermelon or other pretend food was available.

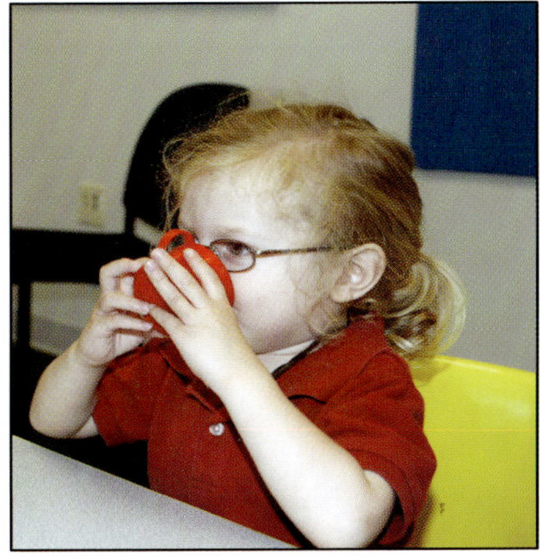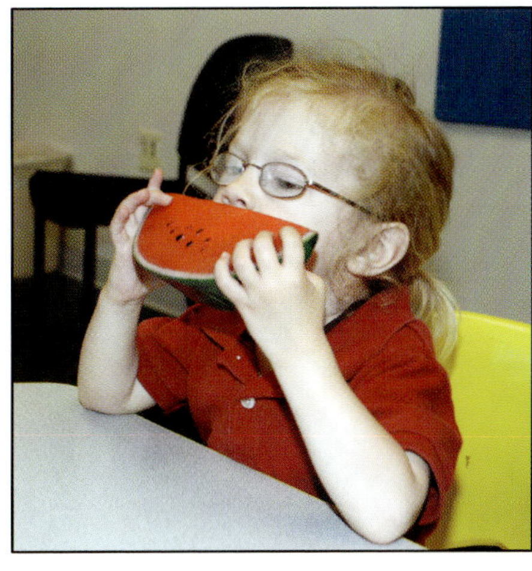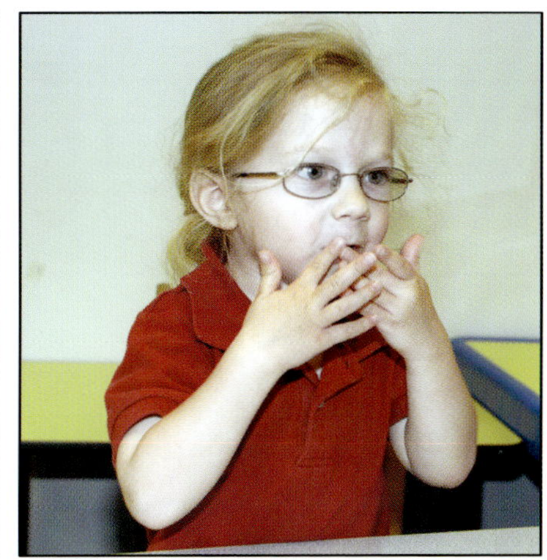

A parent made this game for her son. He rolls the die and pantomimes the action showed. Here, the picture on top when he rolls the die is that of brushing his teeth. Through practice, he learns to pretend as if the toothbrush is there. He acts out brushing his teeth by using his finger as the toothbrush.

PRETEND TO BE SOMEONE ELSE

Children see that objects can become something else, and they also begin to understand how they can become someone other than who they really are. They take on a pretend role or identity. Role-playing usually involves dressing up in a costume related to the role. Most young children love to dress up; children with developmental challenges, however, may need first to become accustomed to wearing something other than their own clothes before we ask them to assume a pretend role.

During hands-on play activities, we often have children wear something special. Here a student wears a big bad wolf hat as she pretends to blow down the little pigs' house, just as she heard in the story about the three little pigs. Combining a fun and meaningful activity with a costume helps ease many students into the idea of dressing up.

Another student pretends to jump over a log and into a lily pond. To help him understand that he is pretending to be a frog, he wears a frog hat and holds a frog puppet. Based on a rhyme he hears frequently during circle time, he knows how a frog might act. Animals interest many children and star in stories, songs, and cartoons; even children with early learning challenges often know what sounds animals make and what actions they take. Animals, therefore, comprise a wonderful category for simple beginning role play.

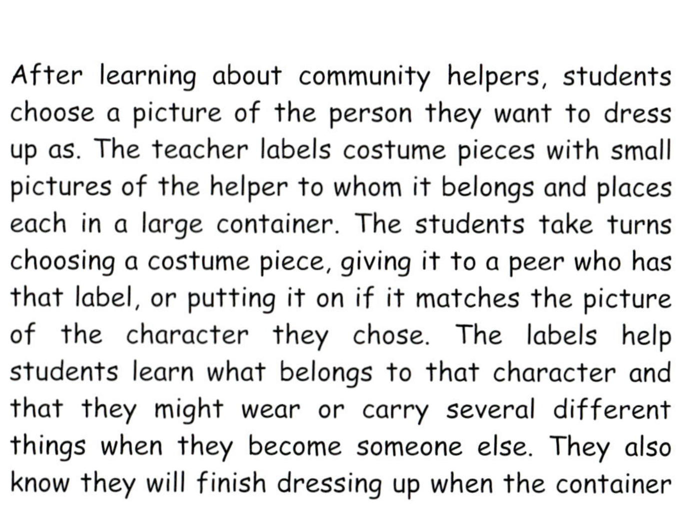

After learning about community helpers, students choose a picture of the person they want to dress up as. The teacher labels costume pieces with small pictures of the helper to whom it belongs and places each in a large container. The students take turns choosing a costume piece, giving it to a peer who has that label, or putting it on if it matches the picture of the character they chose. The labels help students learn what belongs to that character and that they might wear or carry several different things when they become someone else. They also know they will finish dressing up when the container of costume pieces is empty.

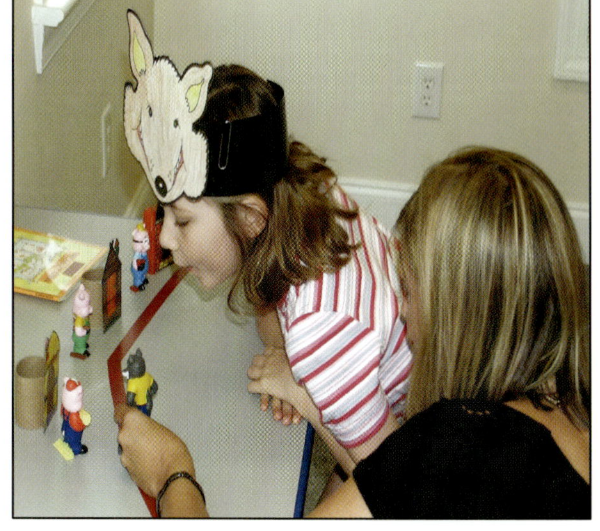

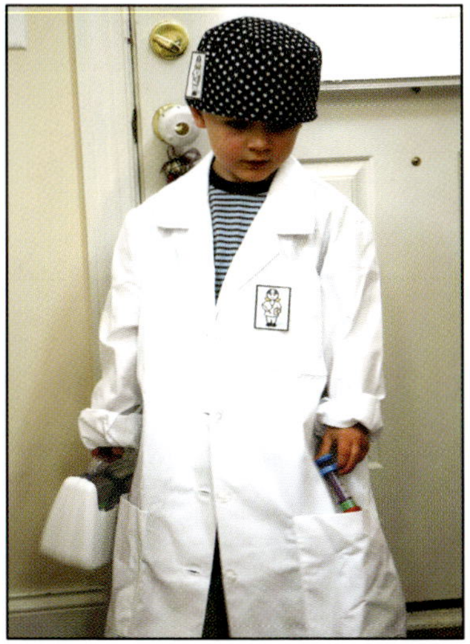

This student really enjoys dressing up but does not always put the costume pieces on in the correct order. For example, the sunglasses, which she puts on first, fall off as the lei goes over her head. Putting the pieces in numbered bags eliminates this problem. The student can then dress up independently and successfully.

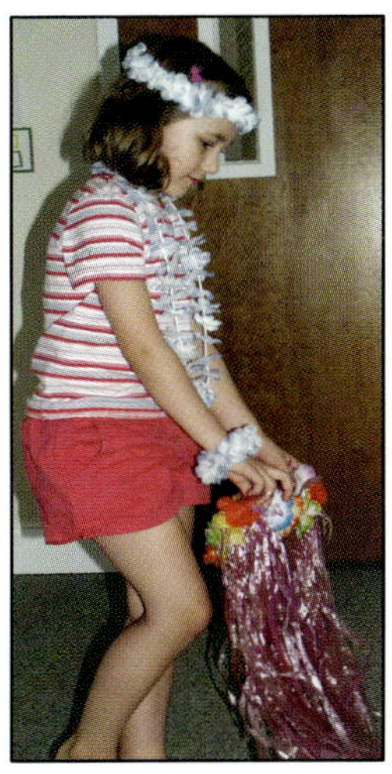

This teacher capitalized on her student's fascination with pirates to develop this dramatic role play. The teacher provides props for the child to dress as a pirate, follow a map, dig, and enjoy the treasure. She engages the student by using her interest and eases her anxiety about trying something new by providing a step by step list of what will happen. A to-do list outlines what will happen and in what order. From the list, the student knows she must dress as a pirate before going on her hunt for treasure. The treasure map provides directions. She digs for what is buried and, then, admires her treasure.

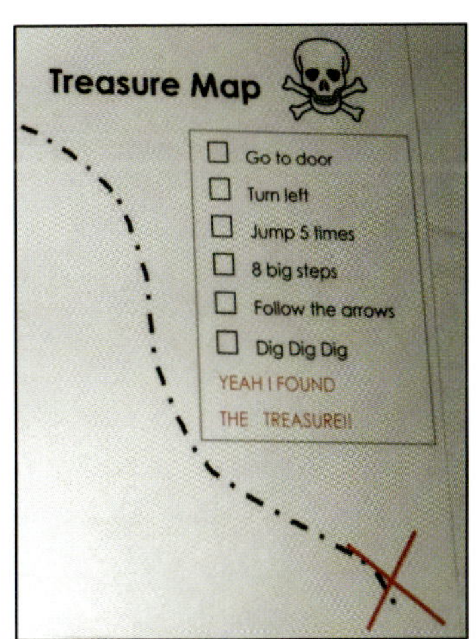

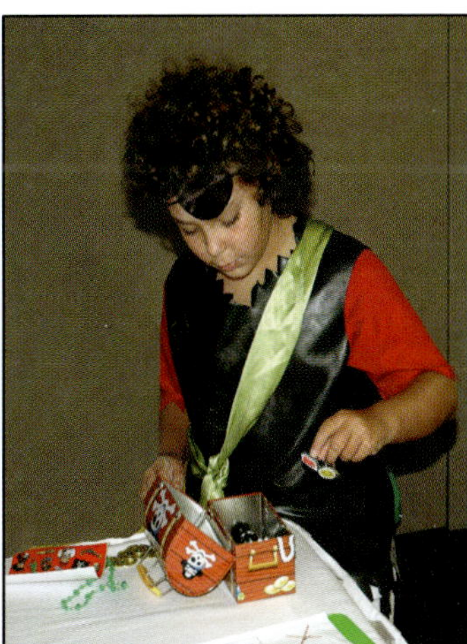

To role play, students need not only to dress as their characters but also to know what their characters typically do. Students in this classroom become cowboys in their pretend worlds. Their teacher provides picture choices of what cowboys do: cook, lasso, ride, feed, and brush the horse. She guides her students to dress as cowboys, choose what they want to act out, and then pretend they are cowboys doing those actions. After learning how to use these visual cues and props with their teacher's direction, they can be made available as reminders in play centers for students to use independently.

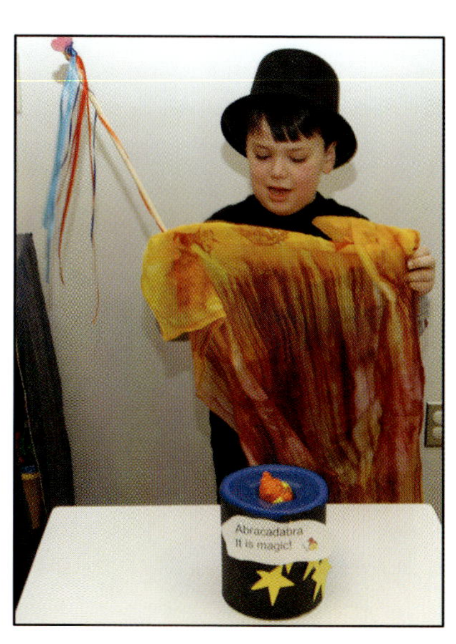

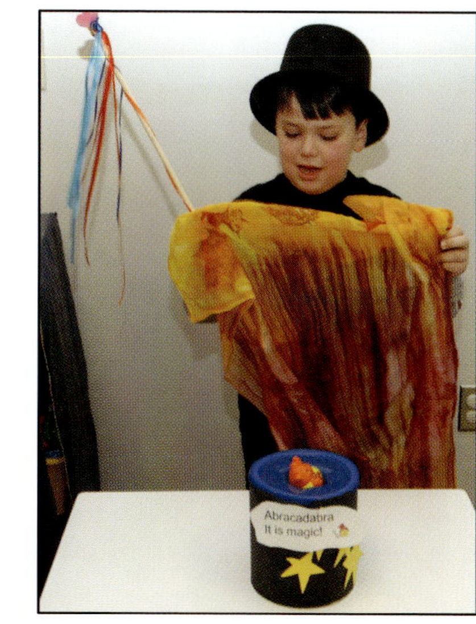

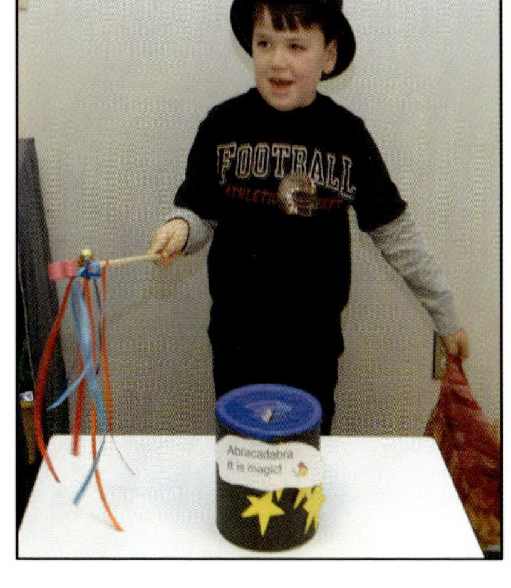

We encourage pretend play and imagination by taking advantage of the experiences the students have and the concepts they learn and find meaningful. This child does not just dress as a magician; he also pretends to do what a magician does. First, he places a toy animal on the rim of the opening of his magic can. He covers this can with his scarf and uses his magic wand to make the toy animal disappear into the can. Saying the magic word, "Abracadabra," adds to the fun, as does the audience's awe at the magical disappearance.

GENERATING ORIGINAL IDEAS

We know our job teaching skills underlying symbolic play is complete when students originate creative play ideas. We cannot teach this ability. We give students the tools and hope they are able to make this cognitive leap from following set scripts to spontaneity and originality. The more we can encourage students to use different toys for the same purpose, to consider possibilities to make a choice, to accept changes to memorized scenarios, and to add their own ideas to structured tasks, the greater the potential that they will begin to think of something different than what they have learned previously.

USE DIFFERENT TOYS FOR THE SAME PURPOSE

Seeing that a different toy can be used for the same purpose is a beginning step in thinking less rotely and using toys more flexibly. In this example, the teacher helps her student understand that he can use many different types of bottles to give the toy mouse a drink.

After the student becomes familiar with the tow truck driver and car driver scripts, (shown previously), we have her use this picture jig to make a car out of Tinker Toys™. We then give her only this car as the prop to drive on the road and crash into the tree. Her acceptance of this new car that looks totally different from the previous toy car she used in the scenarios is a huge step in helping her to think more flexibly about different possibilities.

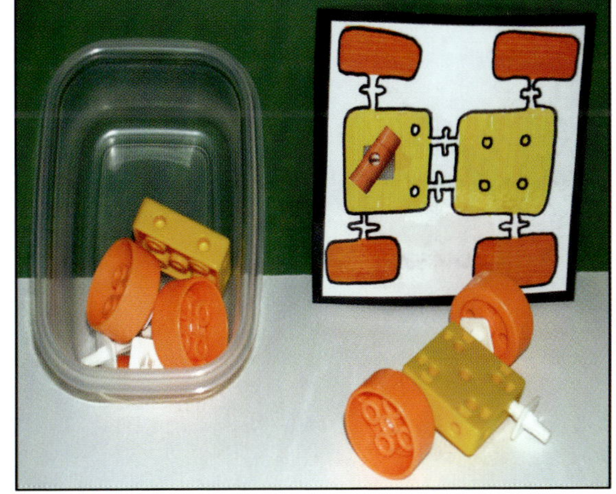

MAKE CHOICES

Students with ASD thrive when we incorporate routines and visual cues to help them play successfully. Within this framework of structure, however we actively have them make choices. Their pausing to consider possibilities is a great beginning step for thinking more independently about what they want to do with toys. These boys circle their choice of an action that they want their toy figures to pretend. They enjoy imagining that their sea animals are chasing, sliding, hiding, swimming, diving, or sleeping in the container of water. Thinking to choose what the animals will pretend reinforces the notion that this play will be symbolic, not just sensory, and increases the likelihood that the students may think of their own ideas during similar play at a later time.

Being guided to make choices while playing helps children think about what to do instead of just following a learned pattern. First, this student chooses which toy from a shelf in a play area. She must decide if she wants to pretend to skate, play with Teddy, dress up as a hula girl, or pretend to be a pirate. She picks dressing up as a hula girl. After dressing up, her teacher presents her with another choice. Does the hula girl want to dance or play the limbo game?

Because children will never accept new ideas or think originally if their ideas remain tightly tied to a set sequence or script, we continually remind ourselves to change the arrangement. We respond to such changes in humorous or matter-of-fact ways in hopes that our students will adopt how we respond, rather than becoming upset. If change with play sequences becomes routine, then the students are more likely to accept when we attempt to change the routines they have established with some prized possesion.

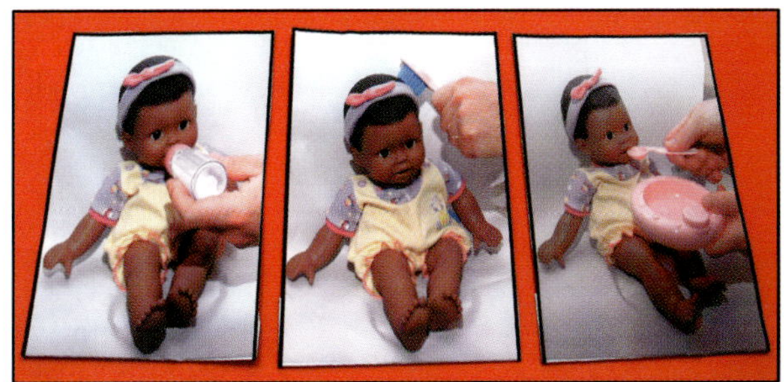 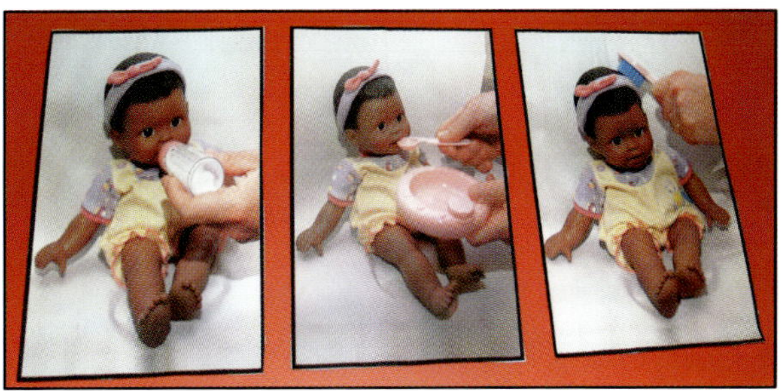 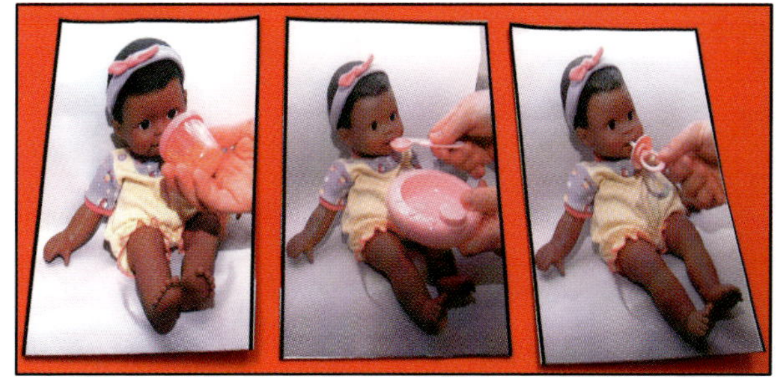

After using a picture sequence to play with baby, we change the order of the pictures, change the actions, or change the props. First, students have baby drink from a bottle, brush baby's hair, and feed baby. Next, we might change the order so that first baby drinks, then eats, then gets her hair brushed. Next, we might change the actions and the props: baby drinks from a cup, not a bottle, and gets a pacifier, not food. We begin routinely teaching the idea of change with play scenarios, such as play with this baby doll, that are not so ingrained. We remember not to make too many changes at once. Once changes in sequences become somewhat understandable and accepted, we attempt to change play ideas that are more important to our students, such as those that may revolve around their interests or that have been memorized from DVDs or storybooks.

In this book about Thomas and Friends™, Percy changes what he says from "Peeeeeeep! Peeeeeeep!" to "Doodle dop!" We try to help students see the humor in this different and silly word, so they do not feel frustrated by the change. In a similar way, we ask children to act out what is depicted in a beloved book. In this example, they pick a card that represents a random page from the book and act out what they see with the characters and props. We encourage them to tolerate that the pages will not be in the same sequence as in the storybook.

INCLUDE SOMETHING HANDMADE INTO PLAY

Young children often include things they make into their play. If our students can learn to do this also, they may decrease the likelihood of rigid play routines. Here, a student is willing to change the looks of the road where she typically drives her toy cars. Using picture models, she builds three different kinds of tunnels. She then pretends to drive a police car through them. If the children use their own constructions when playing in manipulative ways with toys, they may eventually be able to use their handmade items symbolically.

For this tunnel, a piece of white construction paper folds around and attaches to the sides of a piece of wood.

The student makes a different kind of tunnel by stacking two columns of blocks and placing a Tinker Toy™ piece on top.

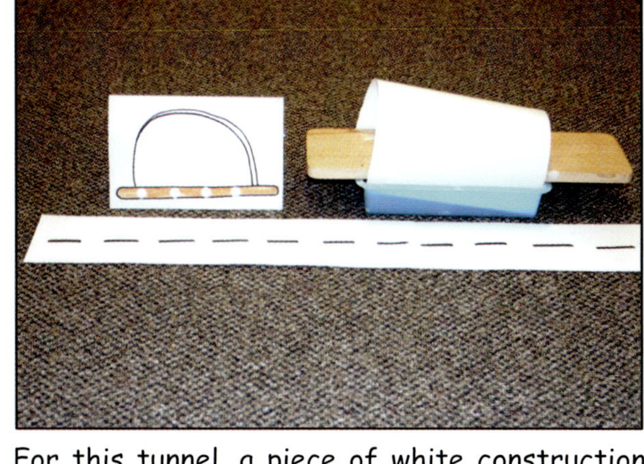

She makes the final tunnel by placing pegs in the board and then an overturned ice tray on top of the pegs.

Students are more apt to incorporate what they make into their pretend play if we choose situations with no established routine. For example, because neither of these students has any set ideas about airplanes, we ask them to make airplanes and then pretend with them. One child follows the picture directions in his teacher-made book. The picture on the tray reminds him to pretend to fly his airplane after he builds it. The second child's teacher shows him pictured suggestions of what he can pretend. Here, he puts gas in the airplane he made.

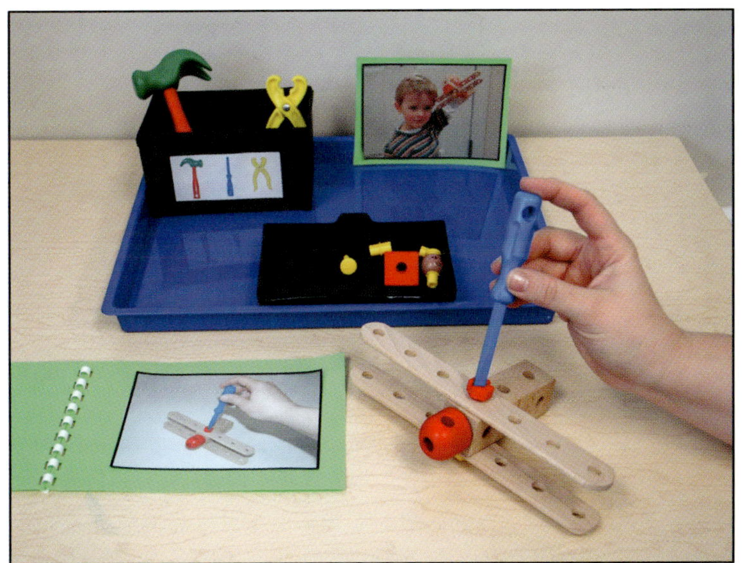

This student uses tissue paper, eyedroppers, and watercolors to make the body of a butterfly. When this is dry, her teacher helps her twist a pipe cleaner around the paper to create the wings and antennae. Her teacher suggests that her student act out typical butterfly activities, such as flying or visiting flowers before suggesting that she pretend something silly that a butterfly could never do, such as swim or drive a car.

THINK OF NEW IDEAS

We embed requests for students to originate ideas within the context of known activities. If we get their minds thinking about certain categories, it is easier for them to think of an idea that pertains to that category. For example, this student is thinking about making a snowman. She reads and checks off the steps involved: body, eyes, nose, mouth, arms, and buttons. Her teacher uses question marks instead of words for the last two steps and lets her student know she is to think of two ideas. Already thinking categorically about what goes with a snowman, she is able to add hat and scarf as the final steps and finds a pipe cleaner for a scarf and a Lego™ for the hat from the container of possibilities her teacher provided.

After following pictured suggestions about what his handmade pig could pretend, his teacher changes the final step on the sequence. Now the student must think of his own pretend idea to answer the question on his list: what can pig do?

Using a familiar visual cue, such as this one that states, "I have an idea," reminds students when it is time to use their own minds to think of something new. We begin using this visual prompt with highly structured tasks during one-to-one teaching times and hope students can eventually be cued to think of new ideas when they see the sign posted in play centers. When we find a visual prompt that a student finds meaningful, we routinely utilize it across multiple settings and situations.

Here, students take turns picking actions from visual choices. One boy chooses a card that shows a dog in a boat and then finds the props to act out this scene. After getting into the rhythm of the game, their teacher slips in a card with no picture; she points to her head and guides them to think of something new the dogs can do. They think of a different idea, having the dogs slide.

   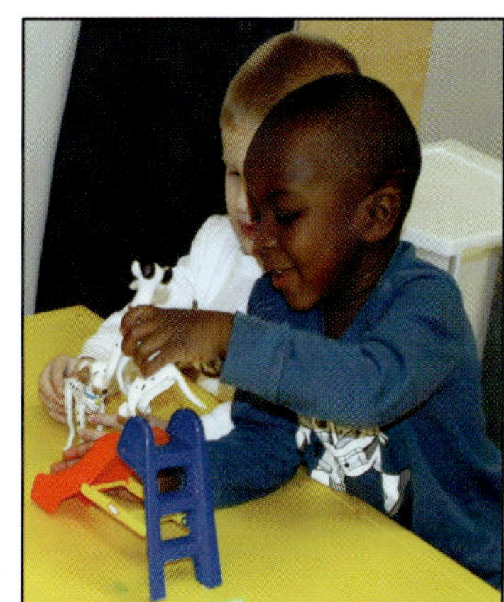

This student pushes his cars through a block tunnel he made. When he was not looking, his teacher closed off his tunnel so no car could go through. Surprised, he looks and smiles at her. She joins him on the play mat and pushes her cars through the tunnel, too. She then encourages him to find something to block off her tunnel so her car cannot go through. He looks around the classroom and finds a cookie tray. He and his teacher share the enjoyment when her car gets stuck in the tunnel. Students who may be capable of thinking creatively may not naturally do so. We, therefore, continually think of ways to encourage them to originate their own ideas.

CHAPTER 6
IT'S A PLAYMATE

Playing with others is so complex. Unlike toys, peers are neither constant nor consistent. While playing, children initiate and respond based on what their playmates do. At any time, a playmate may suggest changes in a turn-taking game or role-playing scenario. With words, they try to convince us to do something their way. They also may tell us, "No," when we ask them to play with us, give us a turn, or suggest a change. Through direct teaching, routines, and visual strategies, we attempt to help our students with these ever-changing interactions. We set up activities, so students can learn how to share, take turns, and communicate with others. Then, we closely observe our students when they play in natural settings with peers to determine what other skills to teach and what routines or cues to restructure. We want our students to experience successful interactive play, so they can see how fulfilling it can be to share and collaborate with playmates. These lessons learned at play become essential social skills useful in all aspects of life.

To help students learn to play with others, consider
- sharing space and materials
  - arrange side-by-side activities,
  - design activities for sharing the same bin of materials,
  - teach how to trade toys, and
  - create times to give pieces that belong to peers,
- establishing back-and-forth sharing times
  - use materials that are easy to share, and
  - provide visual cues,
- giving students practice in communicating
  - request,
  - ask and answer questions,
  - comment,
  - show,
  - initiate play, and
  - share play ideas,
- helping students sustain interactive play
  - organize schedules and classroom spaces,
  - establish classroom routines,
  - enhance role playing, and
  - teach new skills and restructure.

SHARING SPACE AND MATERIALS

There are two essential reasons why we organize the physical play setting so children play in close proximity. One reason is to encourage them to become more aware of their peers. If someone is playing nearby and doing something similar to what we are doing, we often notice and get new ideas. The second reason, we physically structure playtimes is to give our students the experience of sharing space. To occupy close space with peers without becoming upset or withdrawing is a good first sharing lesson. After children feel comfortable with others' sharing their physical space, we begin to create opportunities for them to share materials.

ARRANGE SIDE-BY-SIDE ACTIVITIES

An inflatable swimming pool offers a good sharing space. Here, a student and his teacher sit in this confined space as he plays with sand toys.

Roads, organized by a teacher in a play center, provide a great reason for students to play parallel. Children have their own cars and their own roads so they do not yet have to share materials. They do, however, have to tolerate classmates in a small space. We arrange for nearby play, so our students hopefully will notice each other and accept the commotion that may ensue when sharing a tight space.

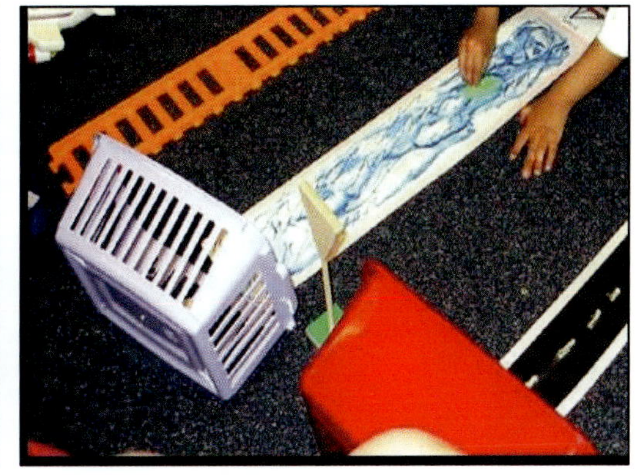

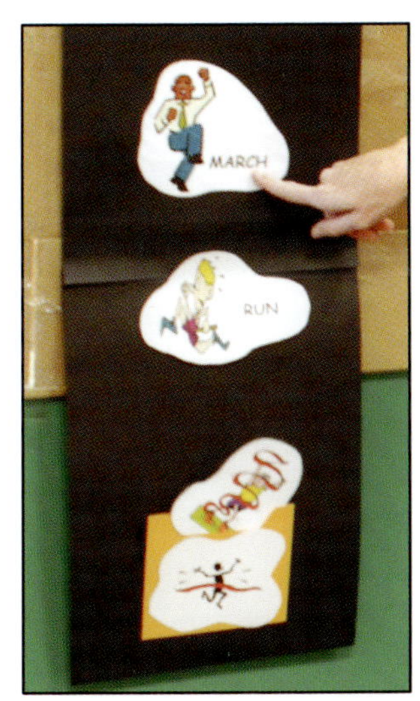

Another teacher changed the movement game musical chairs to "musical share." She points out the visual cues for different ways the children will move while the music plays. When the music stops, each person finds a spot inside a hoop. Because there are fewer hoops than children, students must share the space. This creates another great opportunity for becoming more aware of playmates.

DESIGN ACTIVITIES FOR SHARING THE SAME BIN OF MATERIALS

When we begin teaching about sharing materials, we organize activities in which students have equal access to the materials. There are enough materials for all, so students do not have to take turns or relinquish anything. Instead they share the bin of materials.

The two boys have interests in dinosaurs and, thus, share a bin with dinosaurs hidden in the beans. Although their play is at different levels, one prefers sensory play and the other's is imaginative, they still can share the materials. Both boys can play with any of the dinosaurs, and there is a sufficient number in the bin, so students never have to relinquish one or wait for one.

Three children have a common interest in puzzles. They use the materials, a bin of beans with hidden puzzle pieces and the puzzle board simultaneously. Students put in the pieces they find. They each have a role in completing the puzzle and tolerate having someone else put in a piece. They have learned to share materials when there are enough for all, and there is no waiting.

This student and her teacher share both a bin of bean bags and a bin that is their target.

With her teacher, this student learns about sharing a bin of materials for a common goal. Each chooses a piece and uses it in the train track they are building.

These children share a bin as they make different creations and also share a picture book of possibilities.

TEACH HOW TO TRADE TOYS

We often teach the concept of trading a toy. Trading gives practice in giving up or sharing a toy with which the students are playing, but, immediately, they get another toy in return. The teacher gives her students time to play with toys and then shows them a visual cue that indicates it is time to trade. She teaches what this word means as she guides them to relinquish their toy and accept the peer's toy. Once students learn a trading routine, their teacher can apply it to many different situations.

CREATE TIMES TO GIVE PIECES THAT BELONG TO PEERS

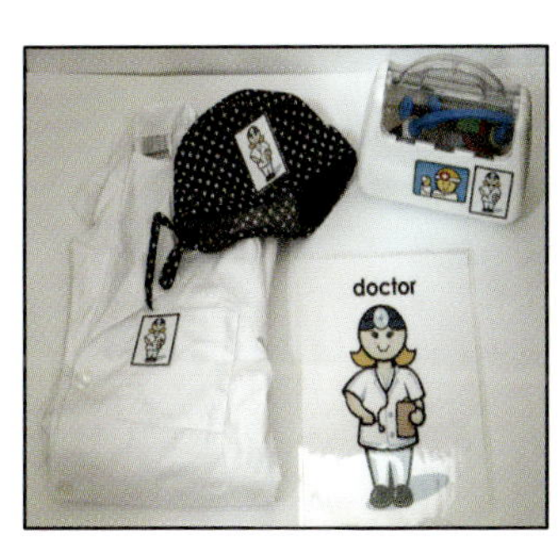 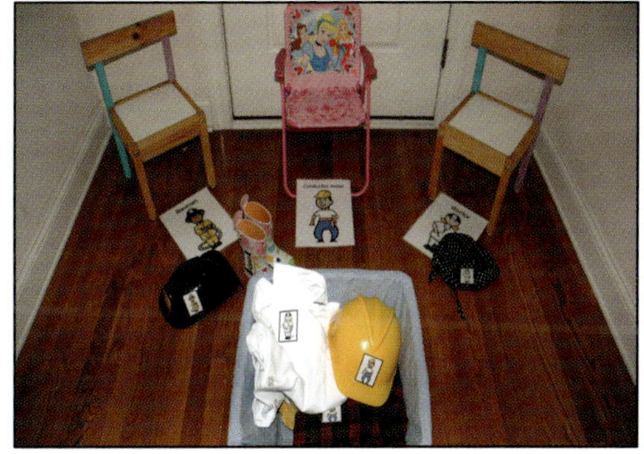

We organize this activity so that students face each other, while sharing a bin of puzzle pieces. We encourage the students to give their peer any puzzle piece that belongs in his or her puzzle. Using the bin of beans as a barrier between the puzzles and using the visual "Give" prompt help the students learn to give up or share a piece.

Similarly, in the activity with labeled costume pieces, children each pick a community helper from pictured choices. Placing the picture in front of their chairs helps them remember their role. They take turns pulling one costume piece from the bin. If the picture on it matches the helper they will pretend to be, they keep it; if it matches their peers' roles, they give it to them.

ESTABLISHING BACK-AND-FORTH SHARING TIMES

Up until now, we have directed our students to share only when there were enough pieces for all or when there was a trade. When we ask them to take turns, they must relinquish a toy and wait for their next turn to get it back. Just as we answered questions about what, why, and for how long when teaching students to play with toys, we try to answer these questions visually when asking students to take turns.

USE MATERIALS THAT ARE EASY TO SHARE

We find it is easier for young children to begin learning about turn-taking within the context of circle time where they have learned to sit and listen. Here, the students take turns playing a drum. The activity provides good turn-taking practice for these students because they like playing it. The drum is an easy toy to give up, however, because the students have no interest in playing it indefinitely, and it is not a prized possession. Also, the end of a song creates a natural finish point. The teacher, too, introduces a countdown routine that can generalize to many turn-taking activities. She says, "Five, four, three, two, one, give," to let the students know when to end their turn and pass the drum to their classmate.

The teacher demonstrates passing the drum when the song ends.

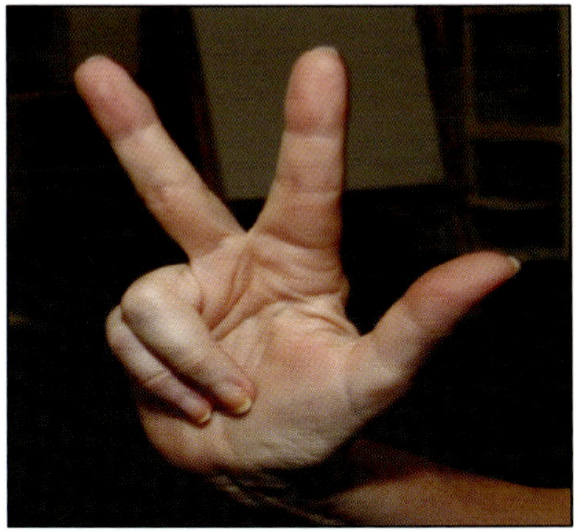

Her fingers show "5, 4, 3, 2, 1, give," the countdown routine.

A student finishes and passes the drum.

The second student plays along with music.

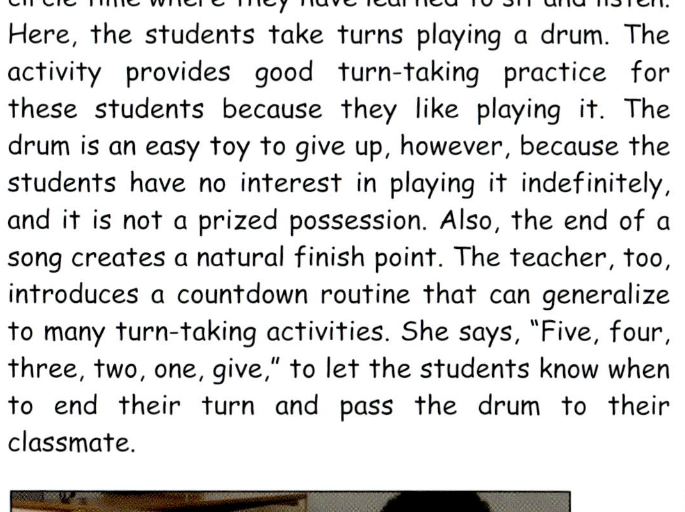

Now it is his peer's turn.

Turns need to be quick in first back-and-forth, sharing activities. In this routine, it is clear to each child what the other child will do: roll the car through the car wash to the end of the road, turn the car around, and return it through the car wash. The toy car wash between the children is a natural barrier that helps clarify that the waiting child's turn will happen again when he sees the car emerge through the car wash. As the students repeat the sequence, they can predict when they will get their next turn. The teacher points to the returning car and enthusiastically encourages her students to watch. She heightens their anticipation and makes waiting more exciting.

 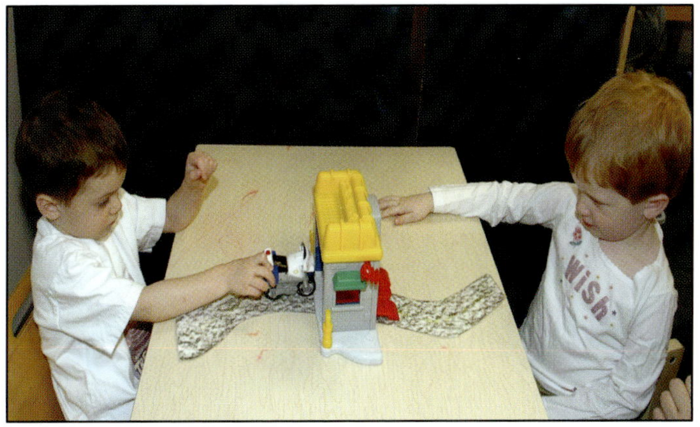

When it is time to share a toy that both children really enjoy, we include more visual cues. We want to help them understand that, although they do have to give a toy up to share it, the peer will return the toy. One teacher created this turn-taking routine to eliminate any surprises. With the black X, she clarifies visually where to put the toy. With the red arrows, she clarifies which direction to push the toy. She chooses a toy with a quick stopping point. Each student activates the toy once. When the spinning balls stop, he knows his turn is all done, and it is now his friend's turn. Once taught, their teacher can adapt elements of this turn-taking routine to different activities.

When learning to share in a back-and-forth manner, it is important to know the meanings of words associated with turn-taking, such as my turn, your turn, and wait. The children can then use these words as prompts to themselves and others about what to do. In this lotto game, children push a can filled with cards back and forth to each other. When the child pushes the can to his playmate, he uncovers a circle with a hand and the word, "Wait". This visual helps the student know that he waits while it is his playmate's turn.

The second game has visual reminders also. Children learn that, when it is their turn, they put, and when it is their peer's turn, they wait.

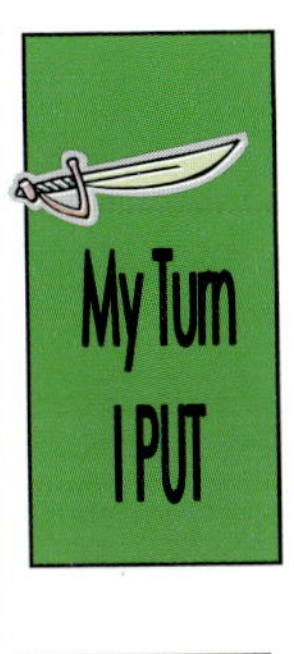

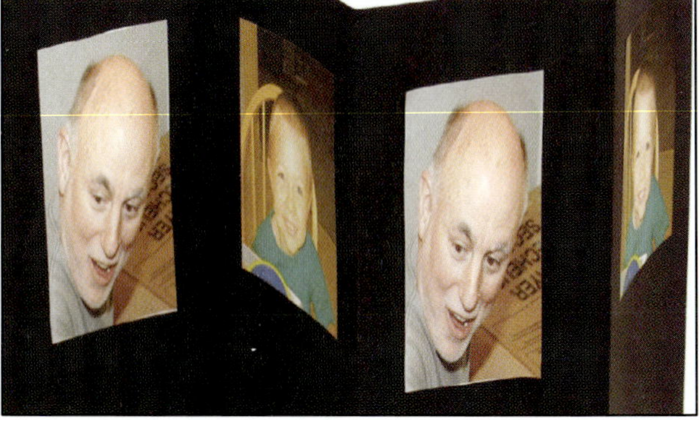

The salient feature in this turn-taking pursuit is not a toy but an activity, stacking blocks. Using visual cues for "my turn and your turn" strengthens students' understanding of these words and of turn-taking in general. When seeing the cards, the teacher guides her students to repeat the words and additionally touch their chests when it is their turn and point to their peer when it is not.

Some students will understand turn-taking best if photos depict whose turn. This visual indicates that the child and his grandfather will take two turns each.

These cues help clarify turn-taking for collaborating on an end result. The student whose picture is paired with cups puts them on saucers, and the one whose picture is beside the teapot pours. Together they make a tea party.

Students toss balls through holes cut into the Spiderman poster. The toy Spiderman head goes underneath the student's picture whose turn it is. To highlight that turns do not happen in a rigid sequence, the teacher varies the order of turns.

Students prepare to relinquish their toy when they hear the verbal countdown and see the visual cue, "5, 4, 3, 2, 1, give." We teach new routines first during playtimes with a teacher and then set up situations between peers where they can use the learned routine. The first student washes her truck with water from a squirt bottle. When her teacher points out the visual prompt, the student hands over the toy. With activities that have no definite ending, this routine and visual prompt make the ending point clear. The boys use the same ending routine when playing with a spin art toy. They squeeze the paint into the tray while they count down to one and then give the tube to their playmate. With repeated practice in a variety of situations, many students will attach meaning to this routine and will use the words even when the visual prompt is not available.

It is extremely helpful to our students to know when their peers will finish a turn. To participate, they need to trust that their classmates will disengage and hand over the toy. We turn to visual cues to help students with the answer. Here, the teacher points to a liquid timer. The student waiting knows when all the colored droplets fall to the bottom of the timer his peer's turn is all done, and he can blow bubbles.

When taking turns with a track, waiting students can look at this visual and know it will be their turn after their peer's car goes around the track three times.

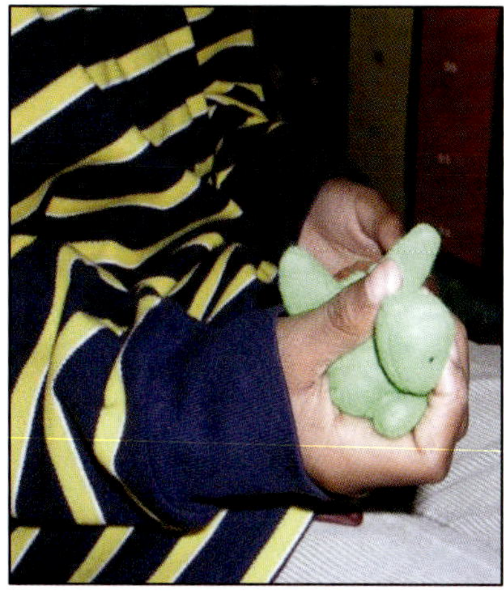

Children are much more willing to wait if they know why they are waiting. Sometimes, however, we want students to be part of turn-taking activities before they understand the concept. They do not mind relinquishing a toy for their peer's turn but may walk away and not stay with the group. Having something to hold while they are waiting often gives a reason to stay, so they can be part of the interactions.

The boys who are bowling wait their turn because this visual reminder answers what they are to do while waiting, sit on their chair.

These students are ready to under-stand that taking turns can be fun social times with friends. With these visual cues, we remind our students to watch while their peers take their turns.

GIVING STUDENTS PRACTICE IN COMMUNICATING

Children talk to each other while playing to make requests, ask questions, give replies, express comments, show objects, initiate play, and share ideas. Many of our students may have large vocabularies but may not use words functionally. Also, they may excel at communicating with adults but not with their peers. Because communicating can be so difficult for students with ASD and other developmental challenges, we design play activities that encourage communication both with caregivers and peers.

REQUEST

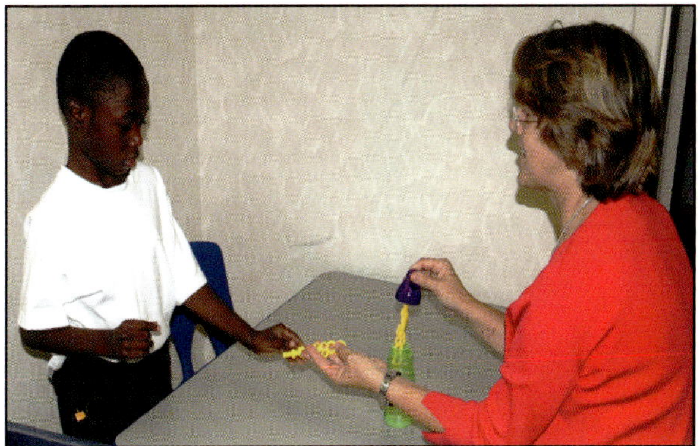

Before expecting our students to make requests of their peers, we ensure they have a well-founded understanding about asking for what they want. For students who do not yet speak or understand that pictures represent objects, we set up situations so they can request by using objects. The first student enjoys seeing a twirling, light-up top. He cannot yet activate it, however, but can learn to give it to his teacher as a way of asking for more spins.

The second student loves to pop bubbles others blow. Here, he exchanges a bubble wand as a way to request that his teacher blow more bubbles.

This student requests which toys she wants to play with in the sand. These cutout pictures are understandable as representations of what she wants. She picks one of them and gives it as a way of making her request known. She first makes these requests of her teacher but later uses the pictures to ask her playmate for the toy.

To complete their coloring, students need specific crayons. Through direct teaching, they know if they do not have a crayon in their cup, they can ask their friend. The children either use the "I need" visual to prompt what to say or give the posted crayon as a way to request the color they need.

Often our students excel at sequencing letters and numbers. This boy displays his ABC knowledge by responding to his playmate's request when she asks what letter comes next. His visual prompt reminds him that a good reply might be, "Here you go." He hands over the letter that comes next and further communicates by pointing out where it goes.

This student has learned to use words to make direct and clear requests in many situations independently. The sentence strip, placed near his board of choices, is a reference that reminds him to get someone's attention by using a name and then letting that person know what he wants. He is also responsible for finding someone to assist him.

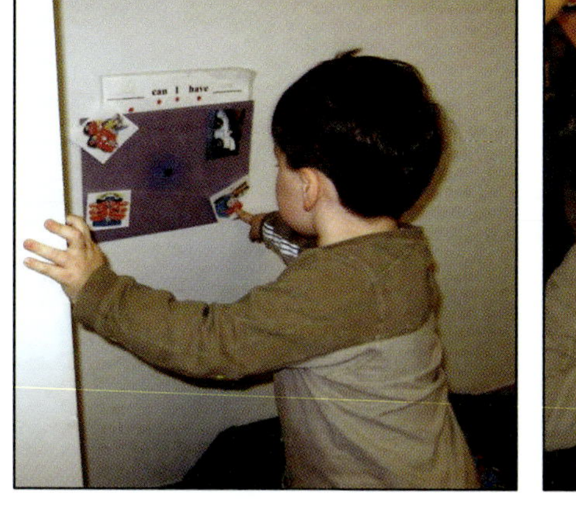

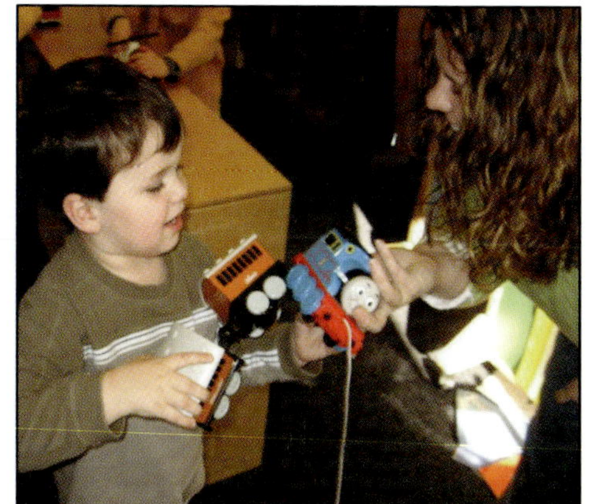

Many children make requests purely for social reasons. Often, before they do something, such as jump in the pool, they ask for someone to watch. Here, this student learns about this reason for requesting. His teacher shows a "Look at me" visual cue that also suggests several actions. The student requests, "Look at me," and then jumps, hops, or dances. Later, he independently decides what he wants his teacher to watch him do.

ASK AND ANSWER QUESTIONS

To help our students answer and ask questions of their playmates, we design structured games with communicative components. As needed, we utilize visual cues to remind our students what to ask or how to respond. As is customary, we first teach a new skill during one-to-one teaching times and have students practice those skills with peers. In this example of a Go Fish game, the teacher and her student first stand their cards up in the box so they can see them but the other person cannot. Between them are the words, yes and no, and colored shapes.   Using the colored prompts as reminders, they take turns either asking for a colored fish or answering yes or no when asked if they have a certain color.

The second Go Fish game uses cards with *Finding Nemo* characters. The students learned to play this game with their teacher, and they now can play it independently with a friend when a visual prompt reminds them to use their friend's name and how to pose the question.

In this game, often presented during circle time, we have one student carry a basket filled with half-fruits. The other students have the remaining halves. The teacher places a student's picture on the clip board. The child with the basket chooses one of the half-fruits from her basket and places that also on the board. The teacher guides this student to ask, "Cassandra, do you have the strawberry?"   She guides the other student to answer yes or no appropriately. When the other half is found, the students put the fruit together.

This adaptation of Eric Carle's book, *Brown Bear, Brown Bear, What do you See?,* is a fun way to answer questions and get to know classmates' names and faces. The children's photos can be interchangeable, so all the students have turns answering the question about who is looking at them. The teacher reads the question to David and then points to Jon who is looking.

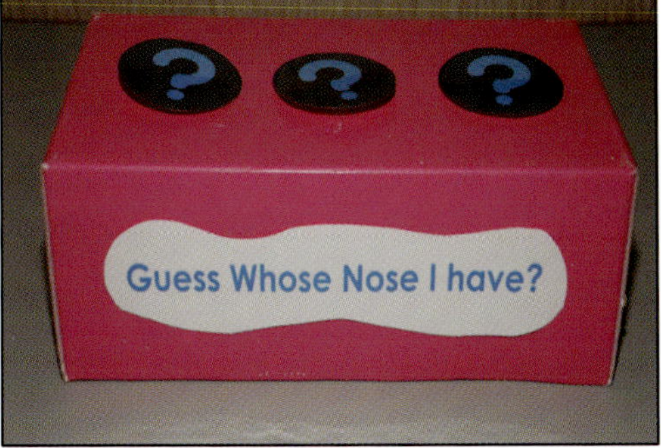

To turn this game, Who Knows Whose Nose, into a questioning and answering activity, we create visual prompts to give students ideas about questions to ask and answers to give. One student picks a nose from a pouch while the other student is not looking and hides it under the box. The child who is guessing sees the "Guess whose nose I have" side of the box. The question marks on top indicate that the children can ask three questions to gather clues about which animal's nose is hidden under the box. More visual cues provide ideas about possible questions to ask: what color, soft or hard, and long or short. The child who has hidden the nose answers these yes/no questions and might use the comments suggested on the side of the box, "You're right! Good job," or, "Bzzz, try again," when his playmate makes a guess.

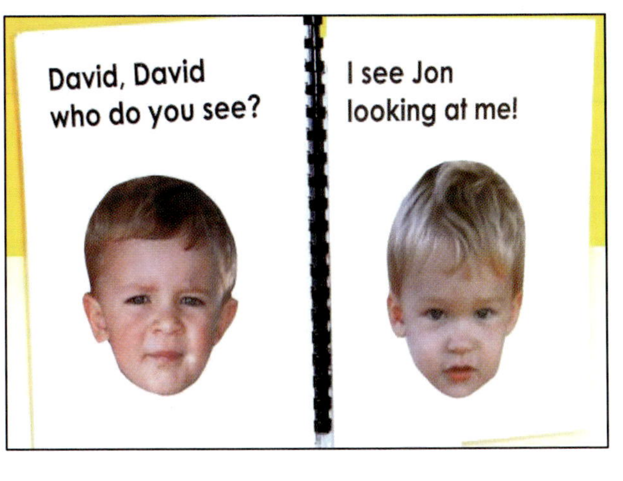

Little children enjoy playing "Where is it?" games. Some of the first questions we might ask young children are where is daddy, where is doggie, etc. Often, before being able to say many words, they answer the question by looking or running to the person named. This game of "Where is it?" uses this student's favorite stuffed animals. His teacher made cutouts of the scanned toys and placed them on a board labeled with the question to ask during the game. The student chooses one of the animals and asks grandfather, "Where is elephant?" He also shows the elephant cutout as an additional way to ask his question. His grandfather playfully hides the elephant toy behind his back to increase social engagement before replying, "Here is elephant."

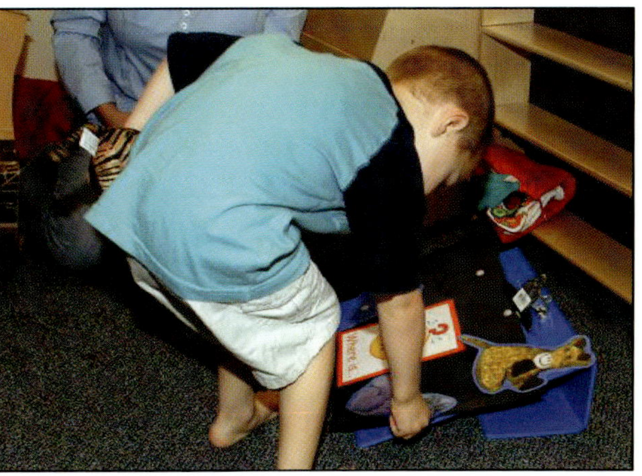

A brother and sister play hide and seek. He must ask the question, aided by the visual prompt, before his sister pops up from under the beanbag.

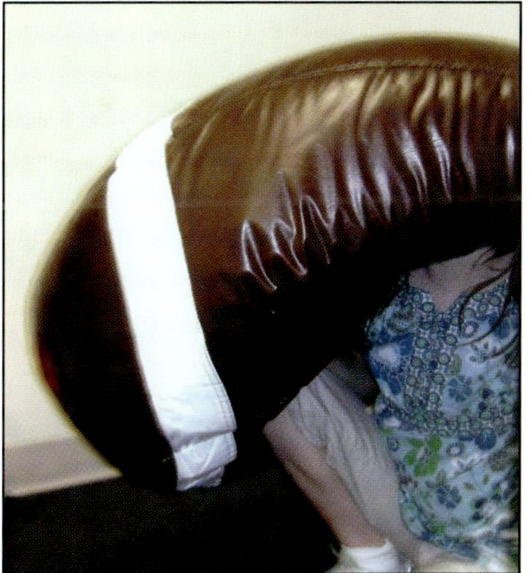

COMMENT

In addition to making requests and asking and answering questions, young children also comment on what they or their friends do. Comments do not result in getting a toy or an answer to a question, but instead result in connecting socially. We structure activities to introduce the idea of making comments and respond enthusiastically to our students' comments to help them understand how social enjoyment can ensue.

The teacher and her students take turns having an animal sticker do some silly action in different rooms of a house. She provides a strip with cartoon characters' suggesting a commenting response, such as cool, great idea, that's funny, or awesome. She models how students can include gestures, such as a thumb up or a high five, with their words. This highly structured game is a fun way to introduce the idea of commenting.

We use this activity with two peers. The first student chooses one of the plastic eggs, opens it, and comments on what he has found. The visual cue suggests a sentence structure to use, "Look, _______, I have a _______." The second student responds positively. The visual cues suggest possible comments. Students learn that comments can tell what we see or compliment what someone else has.

When students benefit from visual cues, we generalize these to other situations. A teacher placed one suggestion for a compliment nearby when two of her students played a turn-taking game. After more practice with these cues, she next placed them in a play center as reminders of what comments friends might say to each other while playing. We locate these visual reminders in places where students more likely will notice them.

A teacher made this watch, model, comment list for her students to teach them how to join in with a group of children. During direct teaching, she taught them to watch what she was playing; next, play with the same toy; and, last, make a comment. She guided her students to use these steps in play areas with peers and placed the visual cue there as a reminder about the strategy for joining friends at play.

Things I might say while I am racing:

On your mark, get set, GO !!!

I'm going to beat you!

Awwww....man, you beat me!

Wow, look at those cars go!

Did you see that!!!

Woohoo...this is fun!!

When another teacher sets up toys for her students, who can read, she includes ideas of possible comments.

SHOW

Many children call attention to something by showing it even before they can say its name. If our students do not naturally develop this social/communicative skill, we actively teach the idea of showing. Because we want our students to take pleasure in showing others, we respond to their social overture in a manner that each individual student will enjoy.

We have our students show their parents what they did at school as part of their daily schedules. Adding a card, "Show Mommy," or "Show Daddy," to their individualized schedules, helps this idea become important to the child. This student shows the car he made during playtime to his mother before he gets in her car. Sometimes children spontaneously will use skills that were first taught as part of daily routines.

Young children often want to share what they find in books with someone else. They point to pictures and want their caregiver to see them, too. Because pointing may not be comprehensible to some of our students, we seek ways to make this communicative skill meaningful. This student and his teacher look at a book together. To help him learn to show her what he sees in books, she includes a finger pointing to red dots on the cover of this book. On various pictures in the book, she places red dots. She asks her student to show her something in the book. Here, she demonstrates how to form a point and then how to touch the red dot. We use children's interests when making these pointing books to augment their attention. If students learn to point out pictures in these books with embedded visual cues, we next try having them show us pictures in books without them.

This student and his teacher take turns choosing and unwrapping presents and then showing what they find.

The teacher places this visual prompt on the table as an additional reminder about what is to happen during the showing game.

The teacher unwraps a present she chooses from the gift box, then enthusiastically shows the toy to her student.

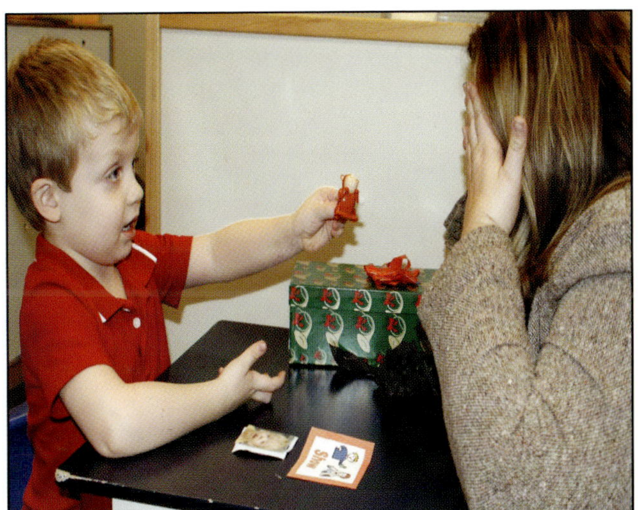

Now it is the student's turn to choose a present. After unwrapping his toy, his teacher touches her eyes as an additional prompt to explain what showing means. The student understands and holds his toy toward her eyes so she can see. After he orients the toy to her, she shows her excitement.

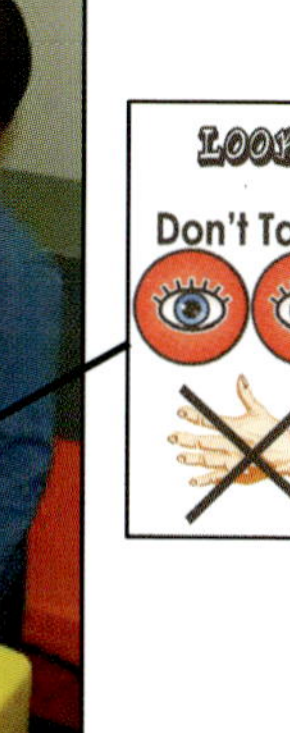

When playing a showing game with these boys, the teacher realized she also needed to teach the role of the person who was being shown the toy, looking, not taking. During the game she added this visual reminder, as well as the one about showing. With practice, the students learned what they were to do when showing the toy found in the tent, and what to do when being shown a toy.

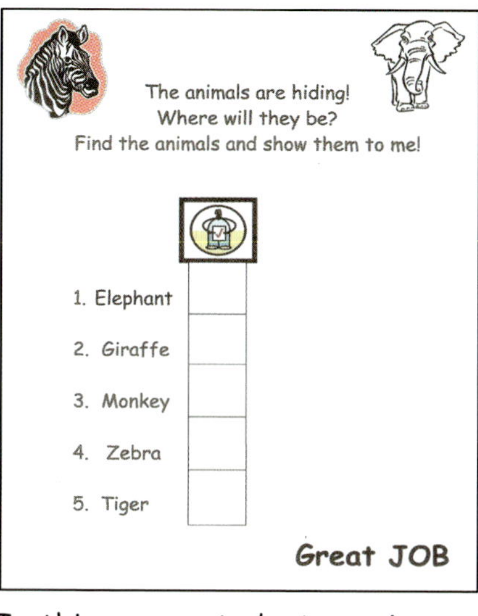

In this game, students again communicate by showing, but they cannot show by directly touching the object. Instead they must show by pointing out what they see in the distance. Animals are placed in different locations within the classroom. The teacher shows a picture of an elephant and points to it while encouraging the students to follow her point. Next, she shows a visual cue card that states, "Show me," and has a drawing of a finger point. One at a time, she reveals pictures of the others animals and asks the students to take turns pointing them out and retrieving them. A checklist lets the students know how many animals are hidden. After each one is found, they check it off their list.

An important reason to communicate with friends is to get them to play with you. Students with developmental challenges may rarely communicate for this purpose because they may not plan ahead, may not have a way of asking, and may prefer playing alone. We want our students, however, to experience playing with others and choosing with whom to play. We begin during one-to-one sessions where we combine our models, directions, and other prompts with visual cues. When the cues become meaningful, we encourage our students to use them independently when we are not there.

Here a teacher introduces a "Let's Play" visual cue to her student. She shows him what it means by having him play ball with her. After using the visual cue in a variety of situations, the teacher places similar ones on toys that the student enjoys. The card reminds him to take the toy to peers and ask them to play with him.

Here the familiar "I have an idea" card is used on a board of suggestions about what children can ask each other to play. Some students may just need reminders about the possibilities; others, however, may initiate play more easily if they remove one of the choices from the board and give it to their peer.

For readers, we may use written words as reminders. In the area where the student builds trains, a favorite activity, his teacher includes written suggestions. Using these, he asks his peer to build one, too.

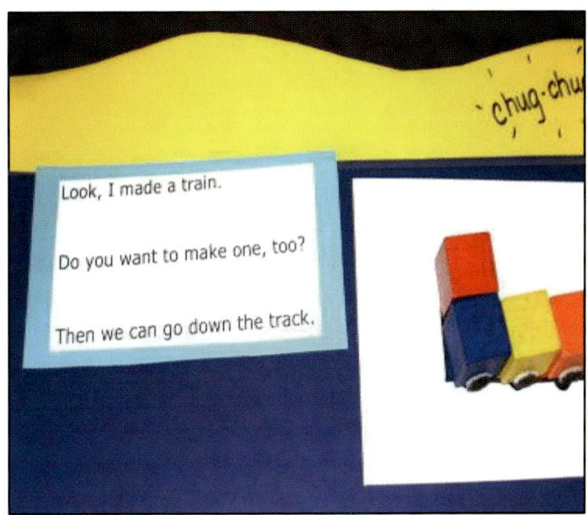

SHARE PLAY IDEAS

Once playing with an activity together, children communicate their ideas about how that play should go. A teacher created a shared drawing activity to give her students this type of experience. She posted open-ended statements and questions to guide the children through the process. The students either take turns telling, asking, or answering by using the script or by originating their own questions and answers.

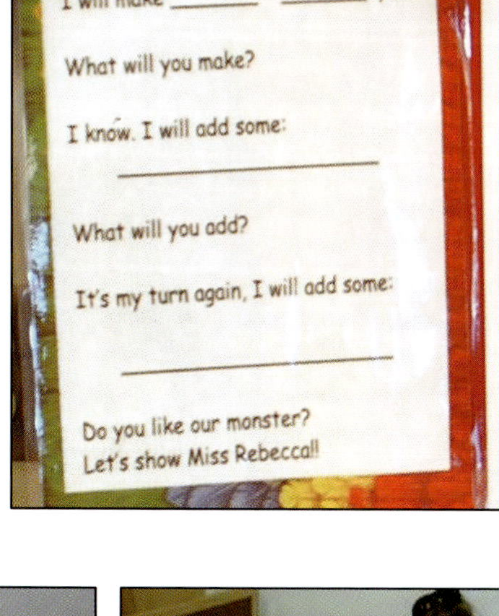

To collaborate while playing, students sometimes need visual ways to help them communicate ideas to each other. These children play together with a toy castle and figures. Their teacher guides them to take turns circling what they will act out, such as ride horses, cross over the drawbridge, or climb the wall. She has the boys show or tell those ideas to each other so they both can act out the ideas at the same time.

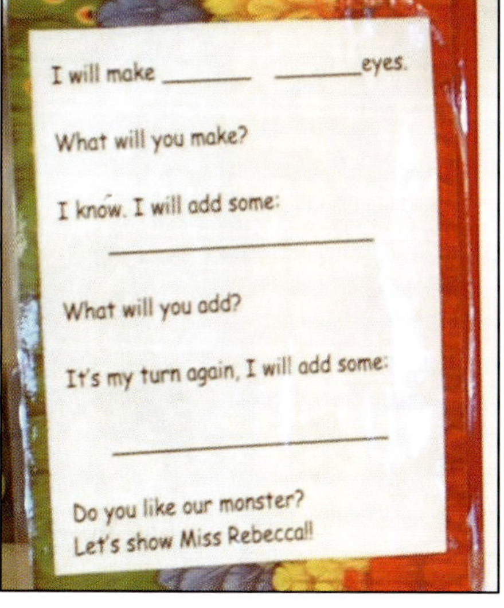

These two boys play with a doll house cooperatively. The choice board to their right gives them a visual way of choosing what they will do while playing with the doll house, such as sleeping, vacuuming, or eating, and a way to communicate that choice to each other.

HELPING STUDENTS SUSTAIN INTERACTIVE PLAY

Now that we have attempted to teach our students how to share, take turns, and communicate with their peers and have embedded visual strategies to remind them of what they learned, we next focus on how we can help them sustain their interactive play. Techniques useful are arranging centers and systems for success, establishing classroom routines that may ease students into letting go of their set ideas about how they play, enhancing role-play, and directly teaching and restructuring after noting remaining areas of need.

ORGANIZE SCHEDULES AND CLASSROOM SPACES

To keep interactions going, we often group students according to their interests, play levels, and temperaments. A teacher knows that both of these boys like to play with cars in functional ways, share them easily, and neither has a rigid way of playing with them. She uses this knowledge to arrange their individual schedules so that they are in the play area at the same time. To maximize their parallel or interactive play, she organizes the area where they will play by limiting the toys to only vehicles and by using shelves to clarify and limit the play space.

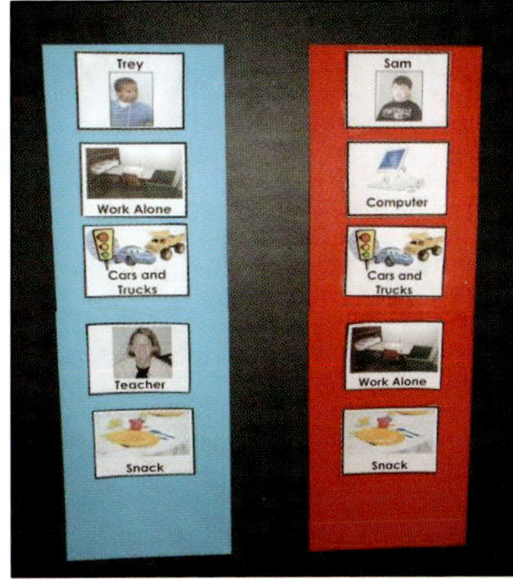

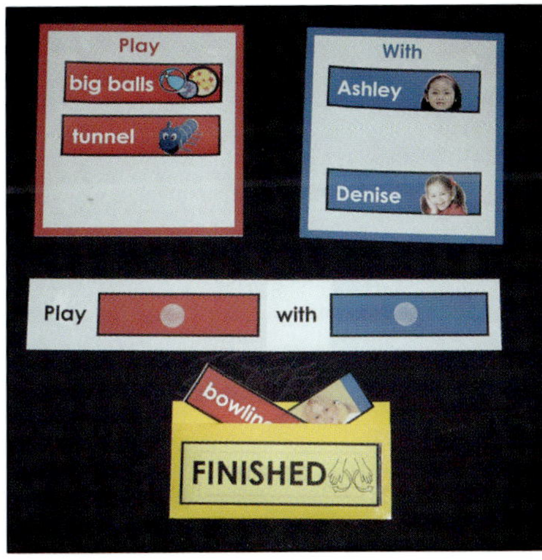

During one-to-one teaching times, another teacher has taught her student to exchange pictures to make requests while playing. She next sets up an activity for the student to request crayons from a peer. For this activity to be successful, she pairs her student with another child who understands the picture exchange and willingly responds.

When we first help students initiate peer play, we want to ensure that the peer asked to play will happily do so. In one classroom, a student working on interactive skills chooses what to play and with whom. The teacher makes sure that the peers listed as choices will eagerly respond.

ESTABLISH ROUTINES THAT ENCOURAGE FLEXIBILITY WHILE RESPECTING PRIZED POSSESSIONS

Play for many of our students halts because they have a passionate interest in a particular toy and may want to play with it exclusively. If we put meaningful daily routines in place that clarify for our students when they can play with their most favorite toy, they may be willing to try other play activities. Also, if we establish routines around turn-taking and sharing, our students learn more about these important social skills.

Effective classrooms have daily schedules that offer both variety and consistency. Following classroom schedules is an accepted routine for most students. Because of strong ideas and interests, students with ASD may not understand the necessity of following these schedules, however, and become frustrated when asked to leave what they prefer. For a schedule to become meaningful, students with ASD often need an individual one that they manipulate and one that specifically shows when they can participate in their favorite activity. Many of our students prefer one center, such as books, over every other one in the classroom. If they learn the routine of following a meaningful daily schedule, however, they will go to other centers.

Here, this boy checks his schedule and sees that he will go to the blocks and cars center. He takes this card to that center and places it on the to-do list which he finds at the entrance. He sees that he will play with cars, builds with Duplos™, and then look at books. While playing with the blocks and cars, he will have opportunities to notice and interact with his peers.

First/next sequencing is a great concept to teach because it is a routine that generalizes to multiple situations. If students trust that we respect their interests and know they will be able to play with their special toys next, they may be more willing to play with something else first. One child was fascinated by trains and wanted to play with them exclusively. Her teacher taught her about first/next sequences, and she was able to play with something else because she was assured train play followed. On this day, the student is to play first at the sensory table with a playmate before playing with her highly preferred trains.

One routine that a teacher established in an inclusive classroom was "have to's" centers and "choose to's" centers. The student sees on his schedule that he has to go to the block center but later can choose to go to a center of his choice. Once in the block center, the student finds bins with cards attached, such as the ones on this container of bristle blocks. These tell him that he has to build a car, a house, and flowers before finding his "choose to" card. Learning this concept helped the student, who was fascinated by trains and only created trains when playing with manipulatives, to play more flexibly, as he more willingly explored new centers and new themes.

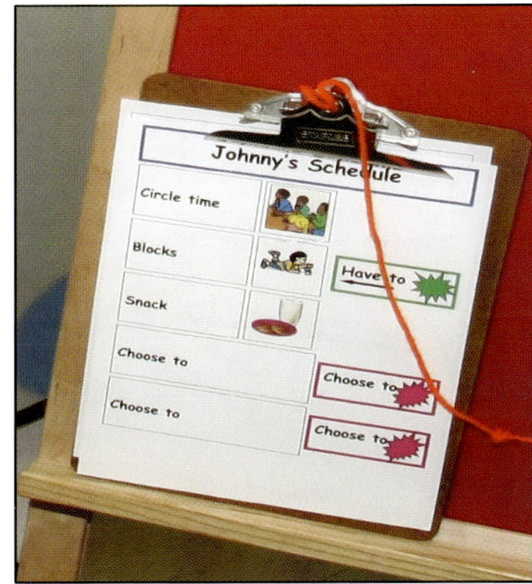

One teacher implemented a sharing routine in her classroom so that sharing happened in a predictable way each day. This routine gave our students, many of whom do not confront sharing because they may not have interest in what another child likes and would never relinquish their prized toys without getting extremely upset, sharing experiences. Instead of show and tell time, the teacher called this routine show and share. After much practice in relinquishing toys and having them returned, children may eventually be willing to let a friend have a short turn with a toy of greater importance to them.

Sometimes we can help students understand that they must play something different if we establish open or closed toy routines. We begin using these types of routines with toys in which students have some limited interest but which are not prized possessions. We use either a sign, similar to this one, or place a cover on the toy to indicate playing with it is not possible at that time.

Favorite toys are difficult for any child to share. Using visual cues to clarify whose turn can help with this social skill. First, we teach routines around turn-taking with toys that are not prized. We would never teach these routines initially with beloved toys. When our students have more understanding about flexibility and negotiations around play, the amount of time they can play independently with others often increases.

At this sand table, children place their photos to show others that it is their turn with this toy. Others who might want to play in the sand know to look for another activity because whose turn is made so clear.

For students who understand sequences and waiting, we might establish a wait list routine, such as the one on this train table. Through teaching, children learn that they may either write their names or place their pictures on the wait list to indicate they will be next. If children learn these types of routines well with non-preferred toys, it may eventually be possible to encourage them to take turns with toys that have greater value to them.

ENHANCE ROLE-PLAYING

Sustained interactive play often revolves around choosing roles and acting them out. For children with developmental challenges, the skills needed for this type of play are daunting. Young children must suggest ideas to each other, negotiate which ideas they will choose, remember what their character might do, gauge what they pretend based on what their peer pretends, and be willing to change when one child changes the theme spontaneously. Luckily, students in a classroom often repeat their play themes. If we see a common role-playing topic, such as setting up a tea party, we think about the steps involved in acting it out. We begin teaching new skills about tea parties in a setting with established one-to-one teaching routines. We supplement our verbal prompts and gestures with visual ones that can be used as reminders when we are not supervising the play. We directly teach the students to utilize these cues.

After learning about tea parties during direct one-to-one teaching times, some students can successfully set up a tea party, similar to what this boy has done. Visual cues are provided to guide him in setting a table. With play set up, he now pretends what typically happens during tea parties: pouring tea, passing food, stirring tea, eating, and drinking. He assumes all roles during the tea party with his stuffed animals.

Here, his friends join the tea party. The child sets up the table as before, but pictures on the teapot and food containers let him know that each of his friends will also have a role. We often use real items in our beginning role play to make it more interesting to our students. Later, we will ask them to pretend as if the items are there. If our students are able to join group play and sustain play because they know the procedure, it has been worth the time we took to teach such schemes.

Because our students often have excellent memories, ideas from stories can easily flow into role-playing. They sustain this type of play because books offer easily recognizable ending points and already are sequenced with roles defined. By retelling stories, our students enhance their early literacy skills.

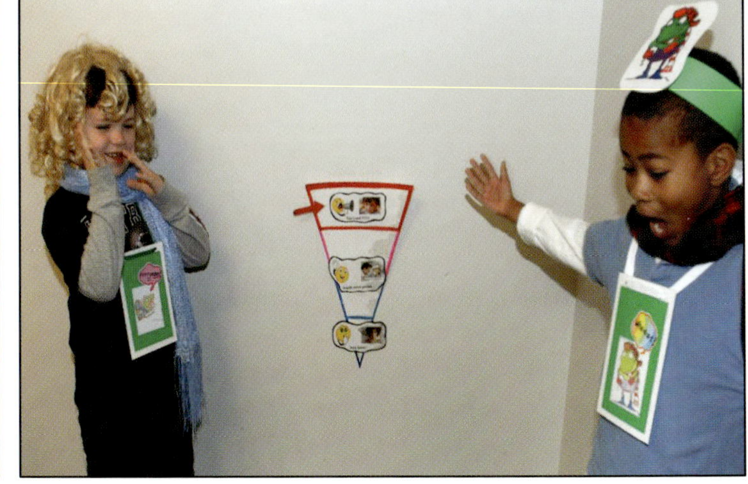

Here, students begin learning the idea of acting out a book script as they blow down the Three Little Pigs' house.

In early learning settings, children often watch and listen as their teachers read to them. This scenario can turn into role-playing with parts for a teacher and a student. By switching roles, children learn this is another situation in which one takes turns.

Here, the teacher provides props for acting out the story, *Froggy Gets Dressed*, by Jonathan London. The wig and frog hat clarify the roles, Mother or Froggy. Because the book has a repetitive story line, the script is easy to recall. Changing voice volume and inflection keeps children engaged and playing together longer. The visual about voice volume lets them figure out if their character talks softly or shouts loudly.

TEACH NEW SKILLS AND RESTRUCTURE

We know that even with the best preteaching, our students will show new areas of need. When we notice these, we immediately identify what new skill the students need to learn. For example, this student excelled when taking turns with activities that had a natural ending but had difficulty finding a stopping point with toys that had no clear-cut ending, such as bubbles. Returning to the one-to-one teaching table designated for practicing new skills, the teacher and her student share a toy camera. To clarify the turn-taking aspect, the teacher pointed out either her or her student's photo. This strategy sustained the picture-taking fun. Once the student replaced his frustration with a new meaningful skill, he was more prepared to enjoy peer play. We recognize that ongoing observation and individualization are key strategies in our efforts to help students sustain play with peers.

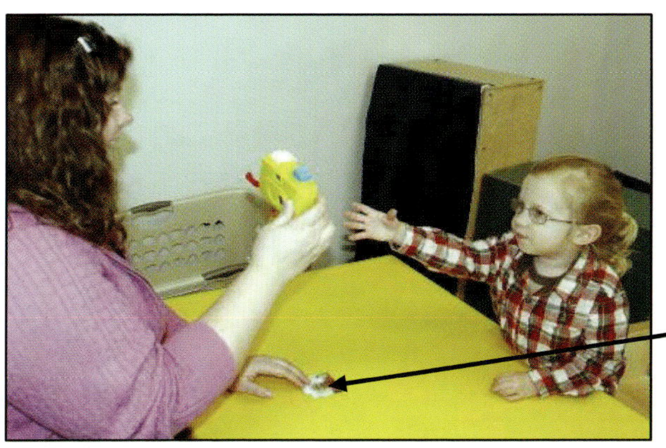

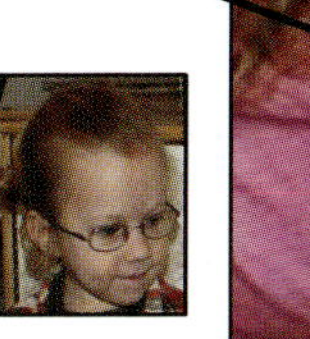

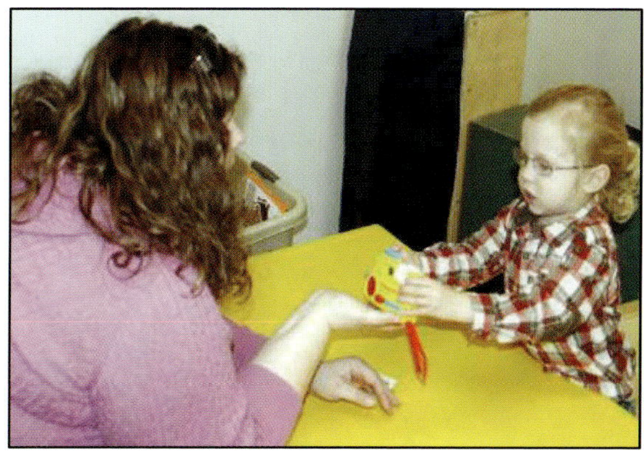

At a teaching table, the teacher shows the picture of her student and indicates it is his turn. He takes a photo and then hands over the camera when his teacher shows her picture and says it is her turn to take a picture.

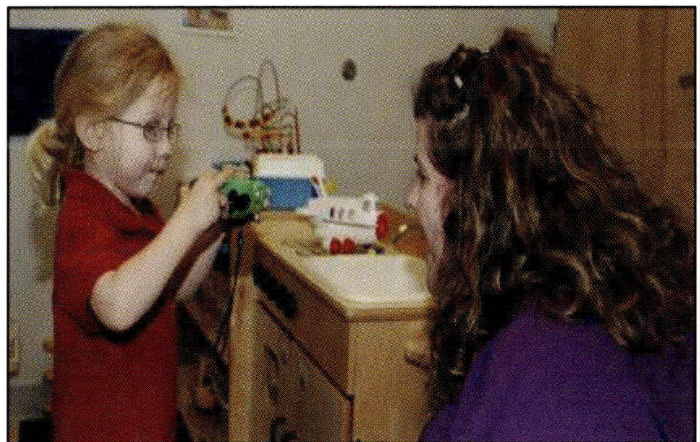
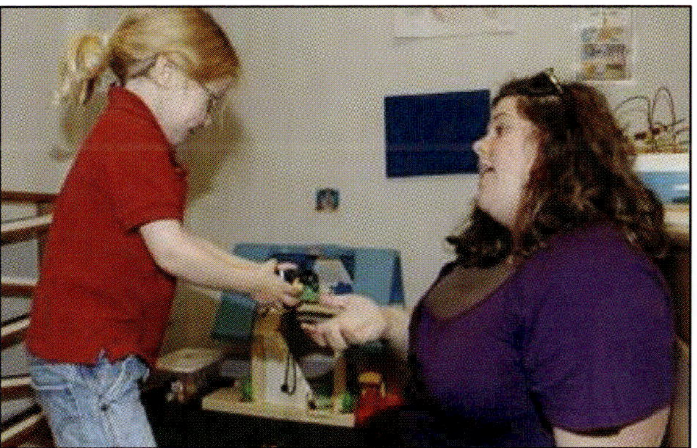
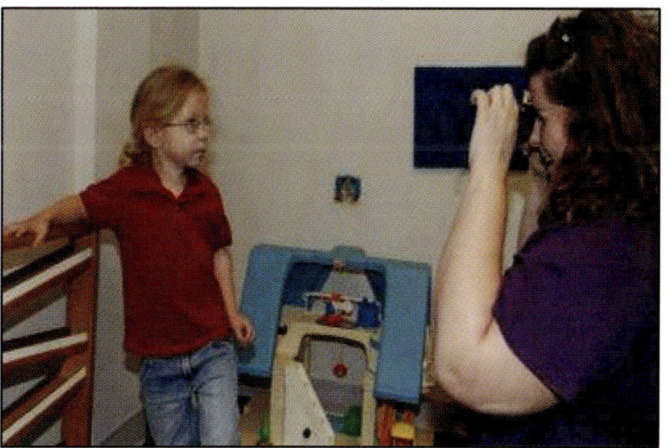

They move to a more natural setting, a play area, to continue to work on this new skill. The student takes his teacher's picture and easily hands over the toy camera and poses when his teacher asks for a turn because these are words he now understands as part of turn-taking routines.

When we notice situations in which play dissolves, we search to figure what new skills need to be taught so that our students can maintain their peer play without becoming upset.

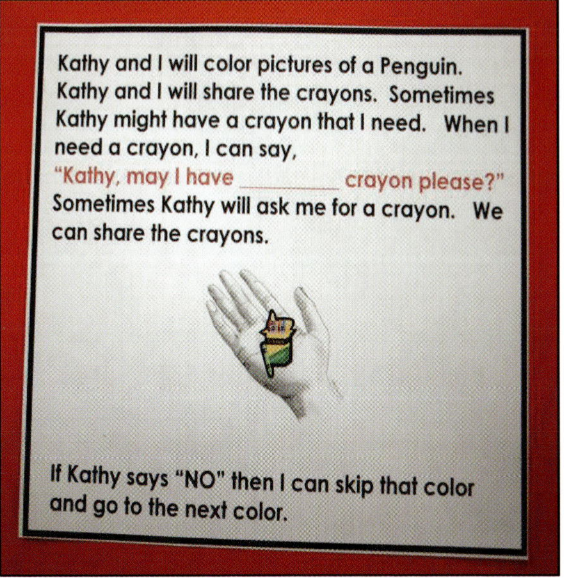

One teacher noticed her student's frustration when a peer denied her request for a shape cutter during a Play-Doh activity. The teacher, then, set up an activity to teach a new skill about skipping or moving on. In the activity, she chose to use crayons, materials of lesser interest, and wrote a script to make the abstract situation more concrete. The student, knowing she could skip a color and go on to another one, learned a new strategy about what to do instead of getting upset.

Some of our students are passive and frequently have their toys taken from them. For these children, we need to teach what to say when someone takes their toys. After one-to-one teaching, however, some students may still struggle to get words out in the midst of stressful situations. Sometimes, if we move the visual reminder closer to favorite toys, students then remember what to do. They can focus on the visual cue during these moments and gain enough composure to say words, "Please give that back."

Other children may become upset when told no when they ask for a turn during center times. Just restructuring the physical setting to create a "Make a Choice" shelf helped some students know that they could pick another toy from this shelf when their peers could not share at the moment when asked. When children know what to do, play times can continue without interruption.

Another student did not want to let go of anything that he made. This interfered with his moving on to play with something else. His creation was very important to him, and he did not want other children to take it apart. His teacher taught him to place his special creations in this box where they would be safe. Making this simple change enabled this student to continue playing because he learned his products would be safe in the "Look What I Made" box.

One teacher developed "What If" books as various social dilemmas arose in her classroom. These addressed topics, such as what if I need help, or what if I want the train and my friend has it. The teacher read the pages to all children during story times, read specific books to students who needed reminders about how to respond if certain happenings occurred, and then placed the books in play areas. Either with her guidance or independently, students refer to pertinent books according to what occurs while they play. These what if strategies teach new skills and provide students with another way to sustain their play.

Children read "What if" books with their teacher.

The pages from the book hang on clips in play centers.

Pages can be organized on a ring as reminders about what if.

Students who are particular about their arrangements may become upset if someone even looks as if he or she might touch the toys. We respect how important their array may be to our students and provide an individualized space within a play area. While this strategy is a temporary solution, with the end goal being interactive play, it may immediately reduce the student's stress enough to allow him to have more attention and energy to give to other routines that the teacher is trying to impart.

We cut down this large appliance box, so that the students can see each other. In time, we encourage the student to leave his special area and try something new with a peer in another part of the play area. He may more likely do so because he has learned that his toys are secure.

Learning to take a break when upset is an excellent new skill that can generalize across situations. Knowing they can retreat to a break area when social times become too overwhelming ultimately can help students sustain peer interactions for longer periods. This teacher organized a sensory center with items to cuddle and to fiddle with. She included the sensory area as a center choice for all students but also encouraged her students to go there when stressed by too much stimulation. Teaching students to take such breaks gives them a chance to relax before once again playing with friends.

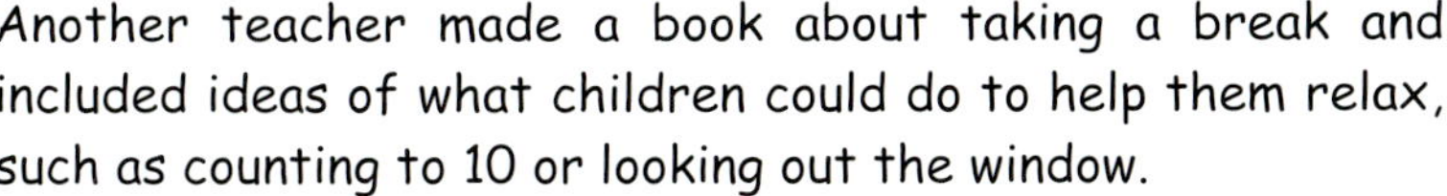

Another teacher made a book about taking a break and included ideas of what children could do to help them relax, such as counting to 10 or looking out the window.

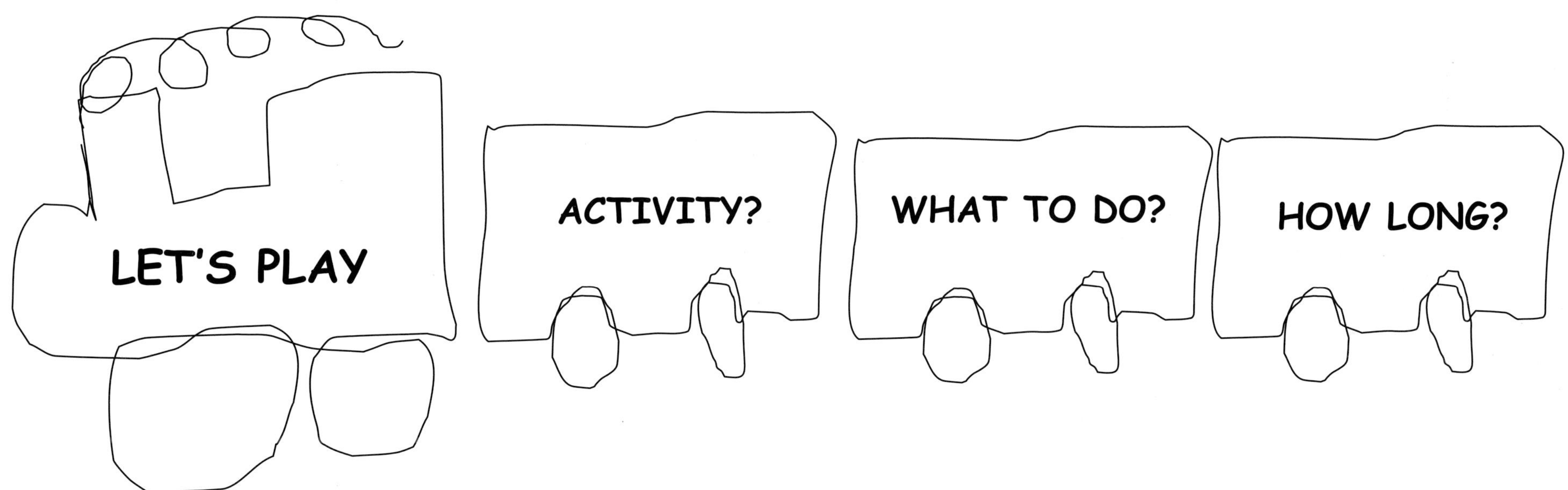

LET'S PLAY
ACTIVITY?
WHAT TO DO?
HOW LONG?

Dried Beans
What?   To pour beans with each colored shovel
How long? Until all shovels are in bucket

Sensory Toys, Feely Can
What? To pull out and explore
How long? Until can is empty

Light Up Squishy Balls
What?   To push balls through cutout can lid
How long? Until bowl is empty and all balls are in can

Water Table
What?   To play with toys in water
How long? Until all toys are used and placed on finished table

Rain Stick
What?   To hear the sounds when turning rain stick to match
            red and blue ends to colored circles
How long? Until each circle is touched, moving left to right

CAUSE AND EFFECT TOYS: Although the toys that one might use to explore can be appealing to children with ASD, knowing what to explore in a meaningful way can be difficult. Clarifying what to explore and the concept of finished often can help the student begin to make cause and effect connections.

Flashlight
What?　　To turn on flashlight, crawl under covered table, and find favorite characters
How long?　Until figure in each outlined box is found

Remote Control Car and Stackables
What?　　To operate control so car goes forward or turns around to knock down objects stacked
How long?　Until all objects are knocked down

Xylophone
What?　　To follow sequence and strike corresponding note/character
How long?　Until each picture is matched, left to right

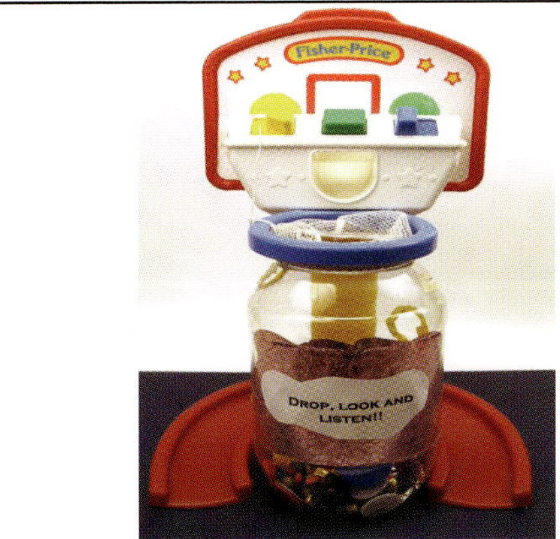

Shape Sorting Hoop
What?　　To hear jingle when pushed shapes hit bells in bottom
How long?　Until each shape goes into container

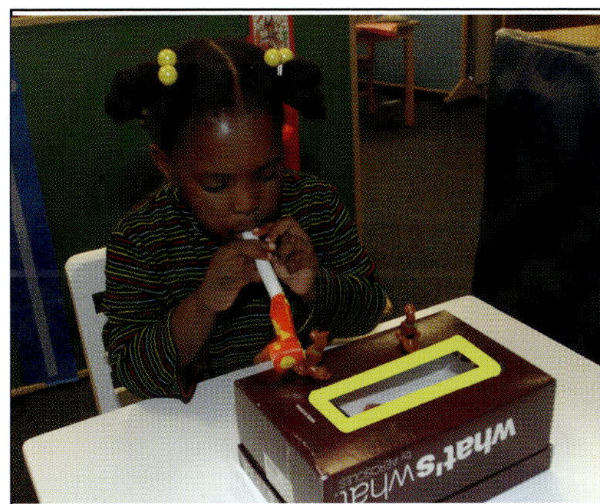

Party Blowers
What?　　To blow noisemaker, hit toy and knock it into box opening
How long?　Until all characters fall into box

CONSTRUCTION TOYS: For some children with ASD, construction toys are appealing because they lend themselves to being sorted or lined up. Constructing can be fun, but first one must decide how to put the toys together in a creative manner.

Stacking Interlocking Blocks
What?   To remove one block from each cup and stack on base
How long? Until blocks are stacked; cups empty

Stacking Blocks That Interconnect
What?   To stack blocks onto blue base
How long? Until all blocks are removed from container and stacked

Blocks
What?   To match colored, shape blocks to picture inside box lid
How long? Until all pieces match picture

Picture Puzzles
What?   To turn pieces to match picture
How long? Until the design on puzzle matches sample pictures are turned over

Cardboard Blocks
What?   To fit blocks inside openings in box and stack remaining blocks on top
How long? Until all blocks are stacked

Nesting/Stacking Blocks
What?   To stack blocks by size, matching scanned diagram
How long? Until all blocks match pictures

BOOKS: Books can be filled with words and pictures that are interesting to some children, but, for others, they hold no meaning beyond paper to eat and pages to flip. Creating routines as one "reads" the book and reasons for turning the pages can add meaning.

Book
What?   To turn each page, remove cover, put shape cover into slit cut in box, look at picture on page
How long? Until each page has been turned and each cover shape removed

Book
What?   To knock on door, open door, and remove object/animal from behind door
How long? Until each page has been turned and door opened

Book
What?   Put sticker on picture in book and say, "Look, I see a __________," using either your finger or teacher-made finger pointer
How long? Until all stickers are removed from bin and put into book

PUPPETS: In addition to offering sensory exploration, puppets are a great toy for acting out familiar routines and activities. Children with ASD often need structure to help them understand how long they should or may continue the activity. Having a clear concept of finished often lengthens the time that a child stays engaged.

Puppet

What? To feed bug to puppet while it stands on table (can inserted into puppet for support)
    To feed bug to puppet while teacher holds it
    To feed bug to puppet while it is in child's hand
How long? Until frog eats all the bugs, and bugs are in bin

Puppet

What? To make puppet jump off log and eat dragonfly; to pull one frog off board and put in box each time it eats dragonfly
How long? Until all frogs are off board and in box

VEHICLES: At first, young children enjoy using vehicles functionally just for pushing about. The children soon learn they also can imagine with them. We give clear visual directions with the hope that our students can move from functional toy play to symbolic play.

School bus
What?   To walk characters on path
             to put them on school bus
How long? Until all characters are on bus

Duplo™ vehicle
What?   To build vehicle, matching to photo,
             and then drive on path
How long? Until vehicles are built and driven on
             path

Garbage truck
What?   To drive truck on road and pick up
             trash
How long? Until all trash is off road and in back
             of truck

Car game
What?   To drive car to location depicted on the card drawn: car wash, store, playground, police station; follow directions found at that location
How long? Until all cards have been drawn

PLAY-DOH: Some of our students shy away from Play-doh activities because they do not like the texture, or they do not have ideas of what to do with the play material. Giving them clear directions about what to do and for how long encourages many of these students to give Play-doh a try.

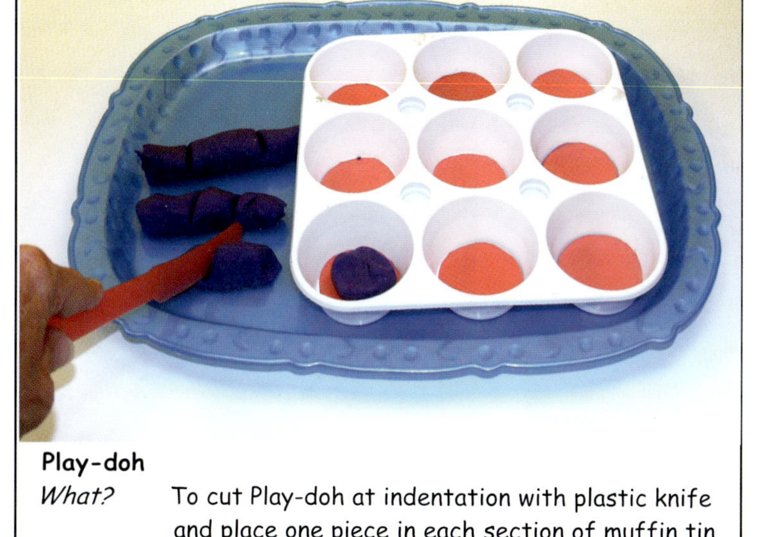

Play-doh
What?   To make Play-doh balls and place on hair bow
How long? Until a piece of Play-doh is on each circle

Play-doh
What?   To make shapes with cookie cutters
How long? Until each outline has a Play-doh figure on it

Play-doh
What?   To cut Play-doh at indentation with plastic knife
              and place one piece in each section of muffin tin
How long? Until there is Play-doh in each section

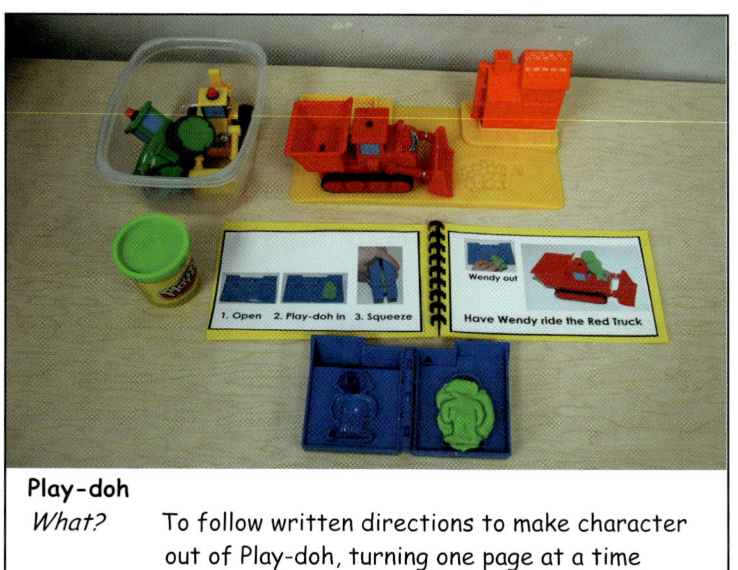

Play-doh
What?   To follow written directions to make character
              out of Play-doh, turning one page at a time
How long? Until all directions in book have been followed

DRAWING AND PAINTING: Drawing and painting play a role in curricula for young children, but organizing the materials and deciding what to create can be problematic for many children with ASD. Segmenting materials, offering suggestions that incorporate interests, and clarifying starting and ending points make these materials more understandable and help the students build a repertoire of drawing skills.

Crayons

What?   To draw/scribble

How long? Until each crayon is used and placed into the cutout opening on right

Painting

What?   To squeeze paint from eye dropper onto paper

How long? Until each dropper has been used and placed into opening at right

Markers

What?   To follow written instructions to draw favorite characters

How long? Until each object has a character drawn on it

Painting

What?   To make apple tree following sample

How long? Until painted picture looks similar to sample

Starting and Ending Points with Markers and Stickers

What?   To match stickers to point, draw vertical line from starting point to ending point

How long? Until all points have been used

DRAWING AND PAINTING (continued)

Drawing

What?   To draw ladybug following numbered instructions

How long?   Until ladybug is drawn and each number is taken off directions page and put into finish box at right

Drawing

What?   To draw parts of a face, using teacher as model

How long?   Until parts of face are drawn

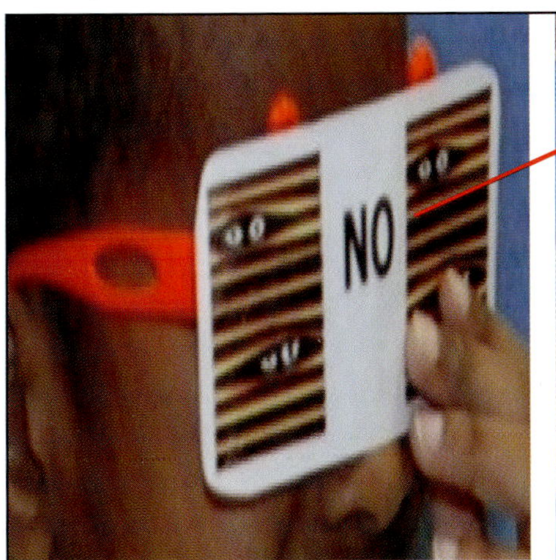

Lotto
What?   To cover pictures on lotto boards with matches and to wear "no-peek" glasses as not to see when choosing card
How long? Until pictures on both boards have been covered

Hide and Seek with Sounds
What?   To take turns hiding while playing musical instrument or finding peer making music (use visual cues to define roles)
How long? Until all musical instruments have been played

Animal Figures
What?   To see what animal is tied to other end when spool/string is pulled from tube
How long? Until there are no more spools or strings to pull

Hiding Cups
What?   To hide and find favorite items under cup
How long? Until turn-taking system finished

SOCIAL GAMES – GIVING: Young children spontaneously bring gifts and soon realize this makes their caregivers feel happy. Children with ASD may not think of this game on their own. They do, however, often enjoy a giving game if we set it up so it is meaningful to them.

Giving Flowers
What?   To find flowers on playground and give them to teacher
How long? Until all flowers are found; one is placed in each section of tray; all pictures are removed from board

SOCIAL GAMES – CHASING: Children love to play chase games, but children with ASD may become overly excited or run from caregivers at inappropriate times, creating perilous situations. The structure of this game requires children to respond to "go" and "stop" signs that can generalize to nongame times when children head out on runs without regarding parent's verbal requests that they return.

Chase
What?   To take turns being runner or chaser (follow directions on go and stop signs during the game)
How long? Until timer beeps

Printable Visual Supports

Enjoy !

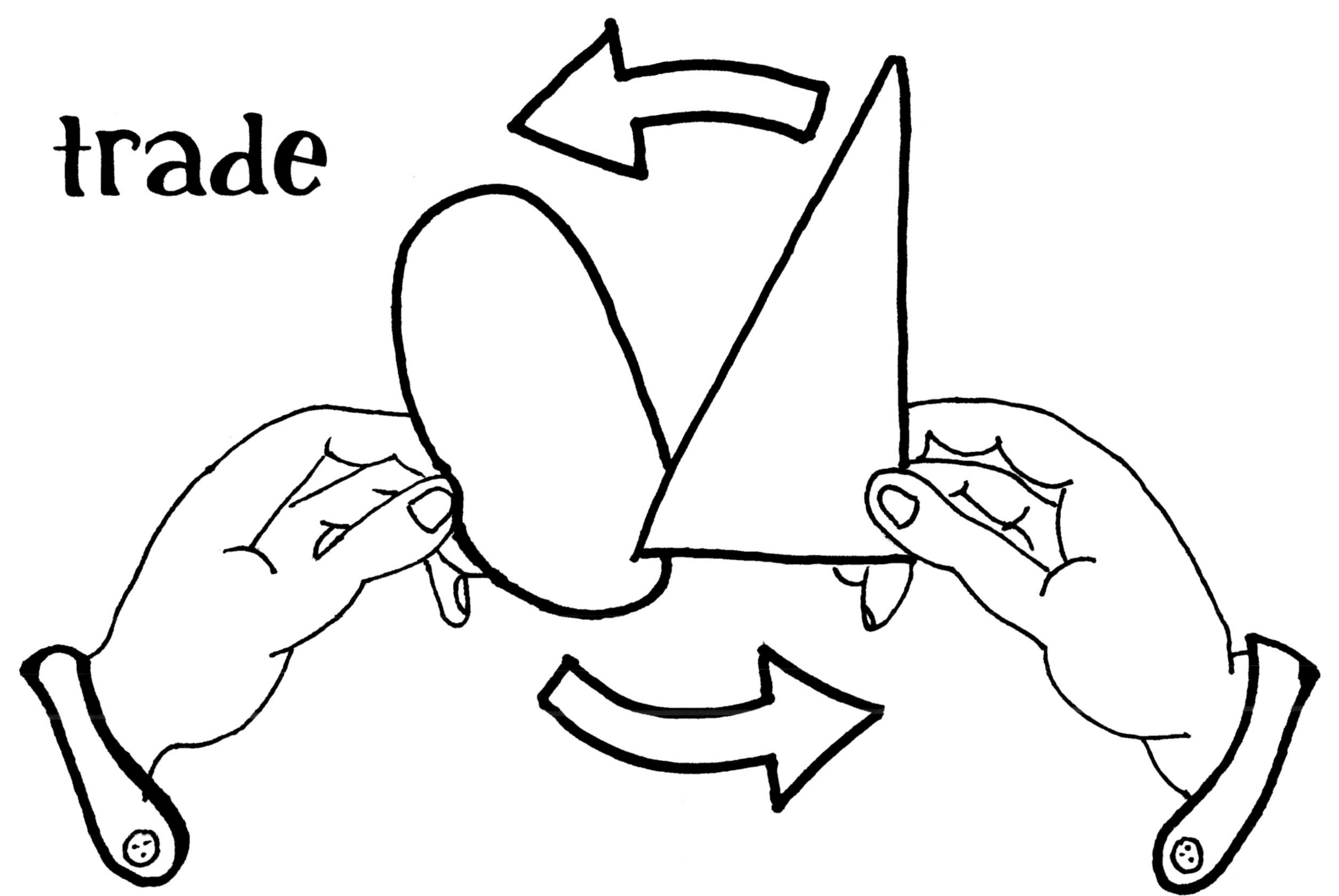
trade

I'll be back
finish later

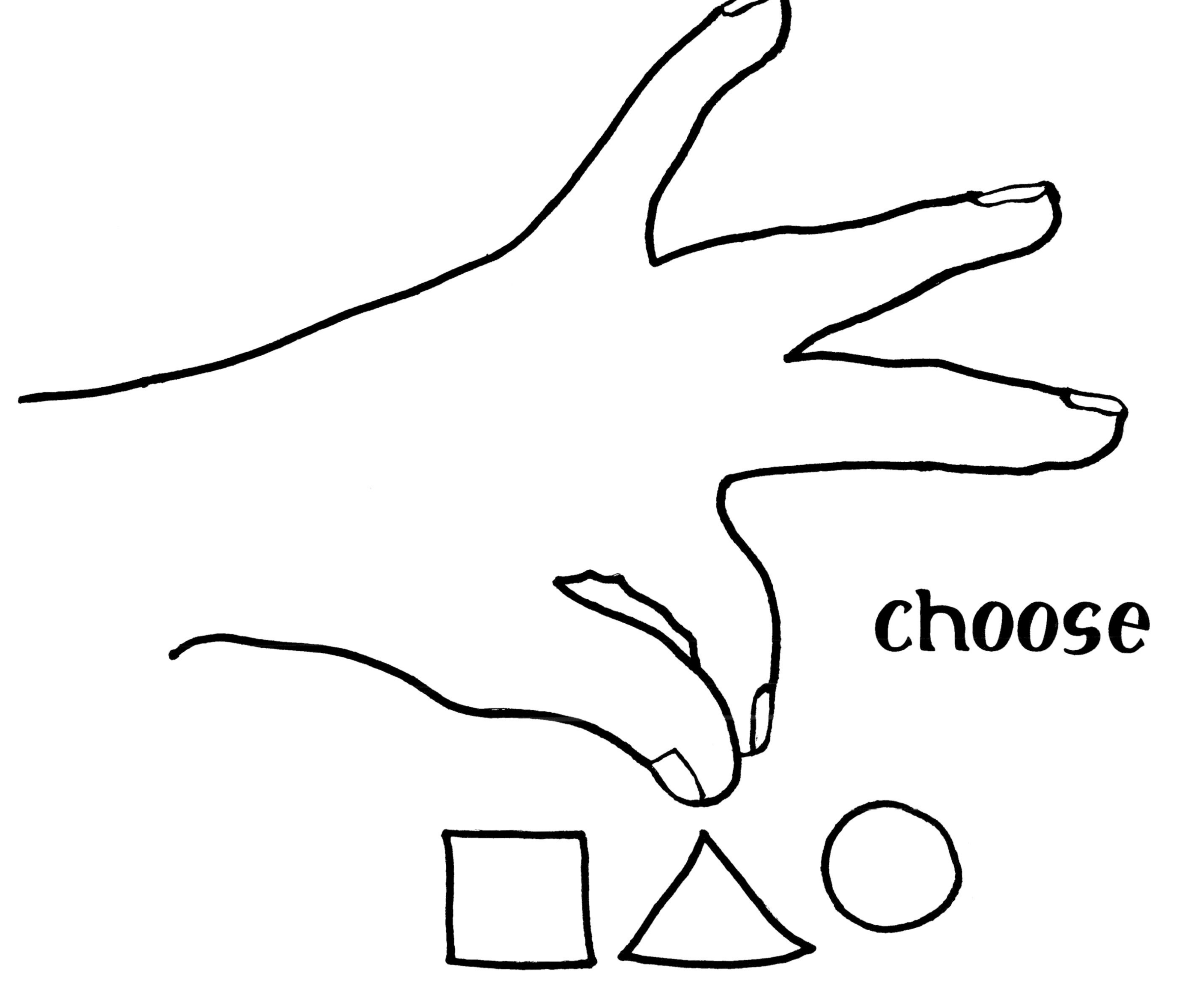

choose

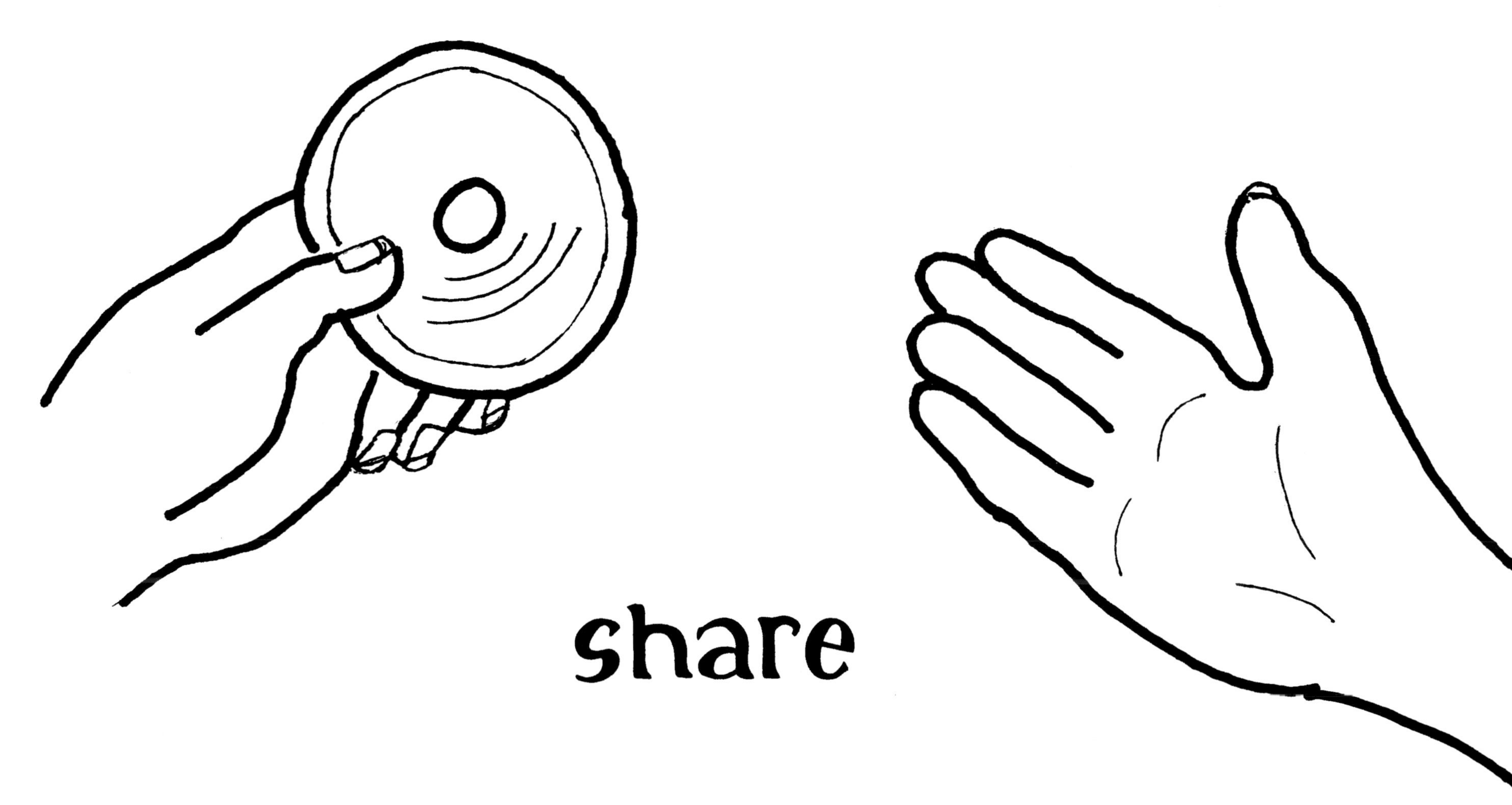

share

I have an idea !

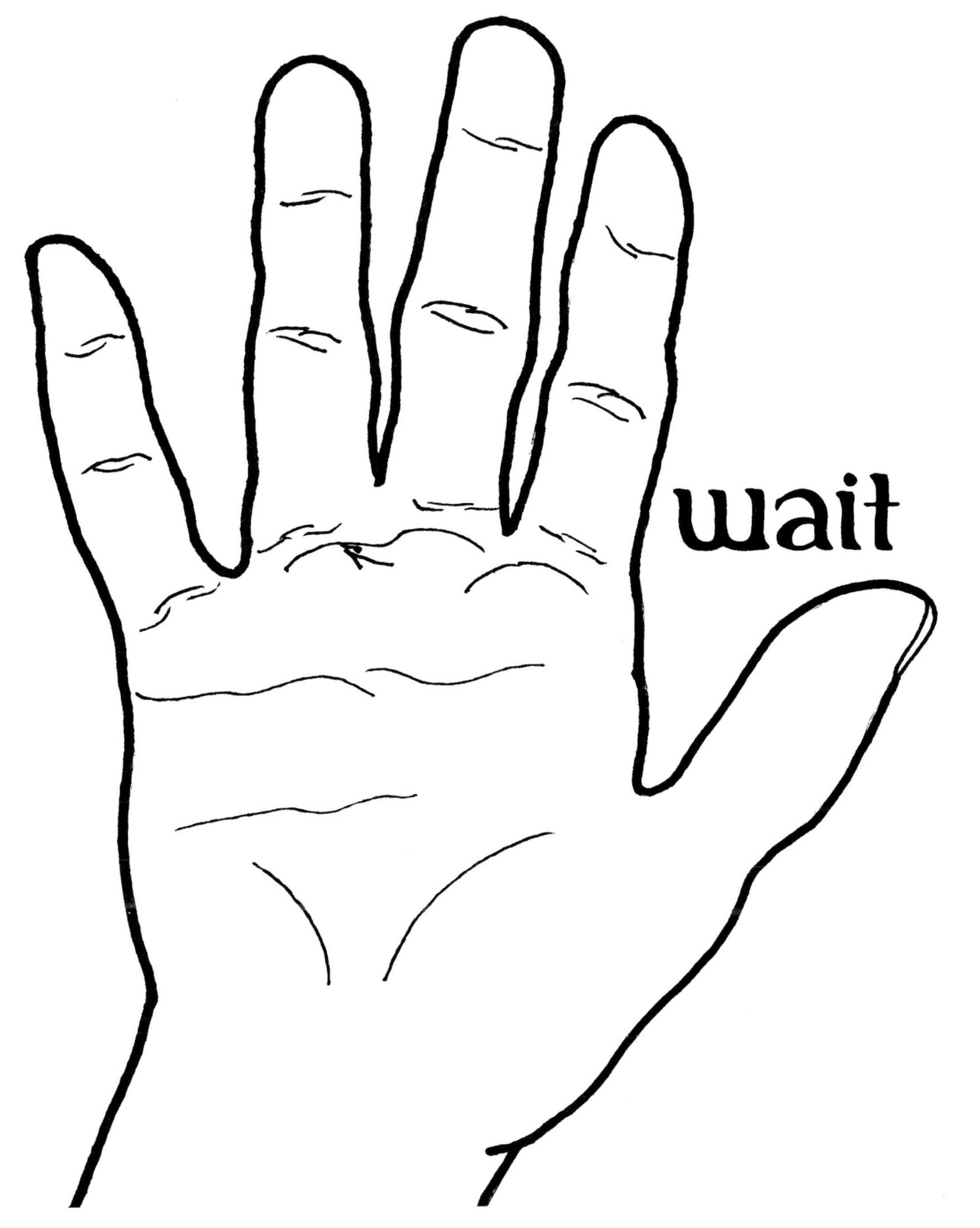

wait

my turn

your turn

look !

great job !!

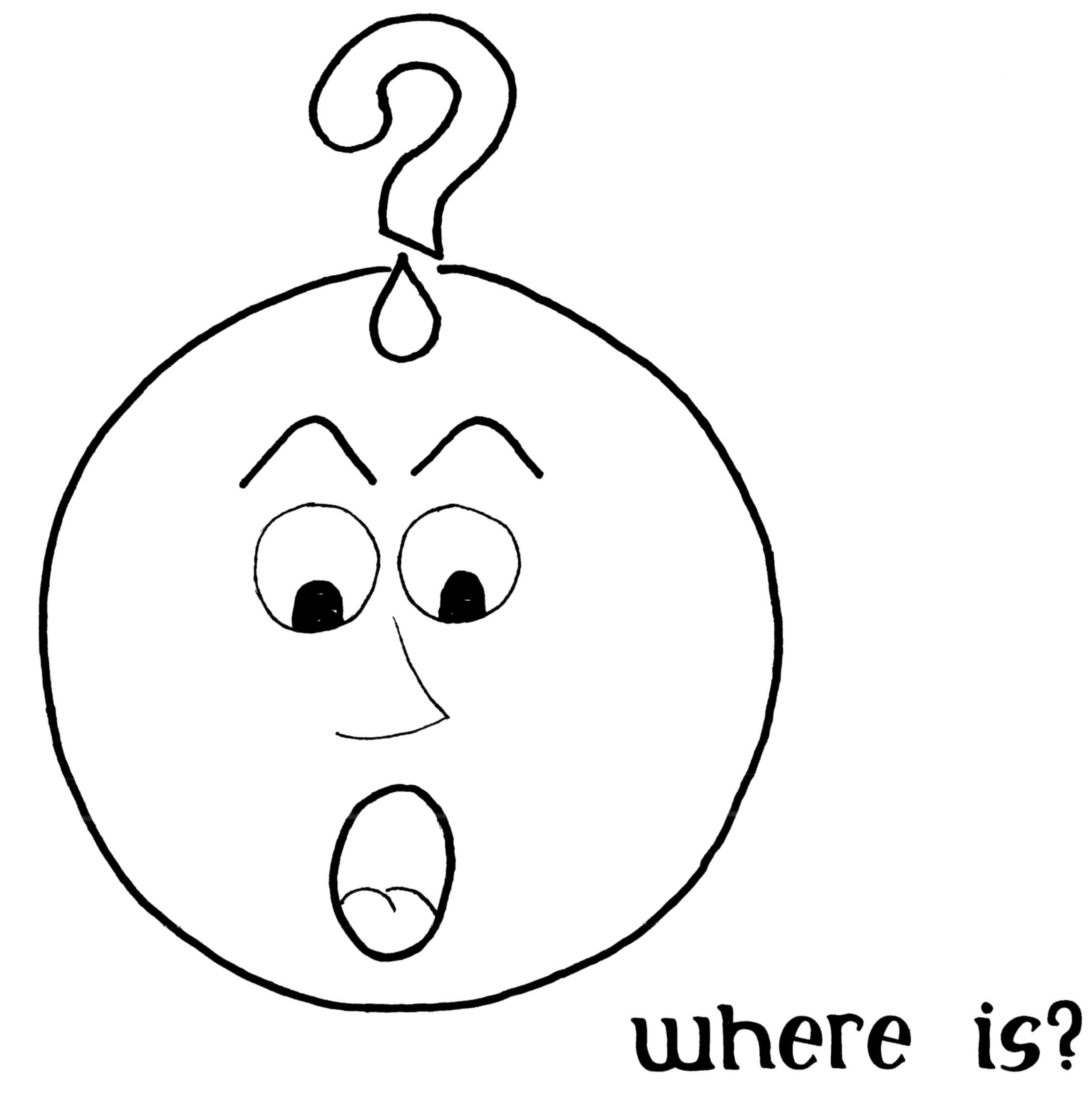

where is?

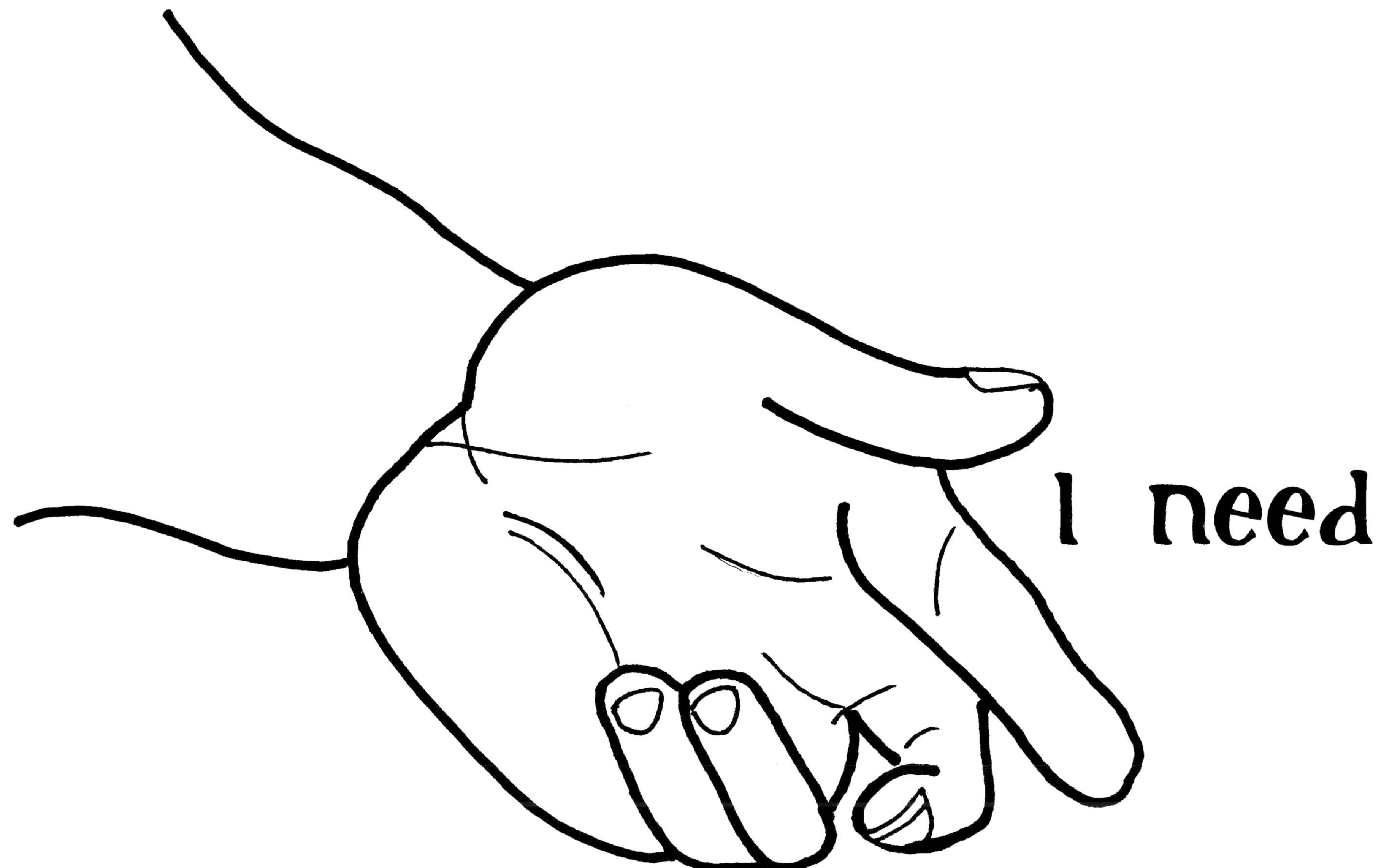
I need

References and Resources

TEACCH

Treatment and Education of Autistic and related Communication handicapped CHildren (TEACCH) is a program at the University of North Carolina which was established in 1965 as the nation's first statewide program for the treatment of children and adults with autism and similar developmental disorders. For information about the services and training opportunities that TEACCH offers, please visit www.TEACCH.com.

Boswell, Susan, Beth Reynolds, Ron Faulkner, and Christie Tanner. TEACCH Preschool Curriculum Guide: A Curriculum Planning and Monitoring Guide for Young Children with Autism and Related Communication Disorders. North Carolina: Lulu Publishing, 2005.

Eckenrode, Laurie, Pat Fennell, and Kathy Hearsey. The Tasks Galore Series. North Carolina: Tasks Galore Publishing, Inc., 2003, 2004, 2005.

Gould, Patty, and Joyce Sullivan. The Inclusive Early Childhood Classroom: Easy Ways to Adapt Learning Centers for All Children. North Carolina: Gryphon House, Inc., 1999.

Kasari, Connie, et al. " Language Outcome in Autism: Randomized Comparison of Joint Attention and Play Interventions." Journal of Consulting and Clinical Psychology, Vol. 76 (2008): Issue 1.

Loden-Talmage, Karen. Climbing Art Obstacles in Autism. North Carolina: Tasks Galore Publishing, Inc., 2007.

Mesibov, Gary B., Eric Schopler, and Victoria Shea. The TEACCH Approach to Autism Spectrum Disorders.
New York: Kluwer Academic/Plenum Publishers, 2005.

Price-Coffee, Juanita.   "The Effects of Structured Play Activities on the Cognitive Development of Kindergarten Children." Dissertation Abstracts International Section A: Humanities and Social Sciences, Vol 56:2-A (1995):0424.
2007.

Larsen, Linda, and Ron Larsen. "Shoe Box Tasks", Centering on Children, Inc., www:shoeboxtasks.com.

Wolfberg, P.J. Play and Imagination in Children with Autism. New York: Teachers College Press, 1995.